THE LOS ANGELES TIMES
PLANNING AND PLANTING THE GARDEN

Robert Smaus

HARRY N. ABRAMS, INC.
PUBLISHERS, NEW YORK

EDITOR
DARLENE GEIS

DESIGNERS
SEYMOUR CHWAST
ROXANNE SLIMAK
FOR THE PUSHPIN GROUP

PHOTOGRAPHS BY
KATHLENE PERSOFF
AND

GLEN ALLISON

GEORGE DE GENNARO

JOHN REED FORESMAN

RICHARD FISH

MARY ELLEN GUFFEY

PETER HOGG

ROSEMARY KAUL

RANDY LEFFINGWELL

JACK NELSON

WAYNE SHIMABUKURO

ILLUSTRATIONS BY
MARTHA AUKLAND

CHRISTINA GIESENFELD

SUSAN RAGSDALE

Library of Congress
Cataloging-in-Publication Data

Smaus, Robert.
Los Angeles Times planning and planting the garden/by Robert Smaus.
p. cm.
ISBN 0–8109–1189–2
1. Landscape gardening. 2. Landscape gardening–California. I. Los Angeles Times. II. Title. III. Title: Planning and planting the garden.
SB473.S543   1989
635.9—dc19   89–6479

CONTENTS

WHAT MAKES A GARDEN?
8
The Possibilities 10
Garden Visit: The Secret Garden 11
Where to Begin: The Notebook 16
Climate and Location 17
Light 19
Shadows and Shade 21

FROM THE GROUND UP
24
The Importance of Paths 26
Garden Visit: A Formal Plan for Roses 31
Garden Visit: An Informal Plan 33
Paving Possibilities 35
Lawns, Patios, and Other Open Spaces 36
Ground Covers and Other Options 40
Garden Visit: No Lawn at All 42

BUILDING THE BACKGROUND
44
A Frame for the Garden 46
Garden Visit: All the Ingredients 48
Keep It Simple and Leave Enough Room 53
Perspective, Proportion, Balance, and the
Rule of Three's and Five's 54
Accent and Surprise 57
Plant Portrait: Those Towering
Delphiniums 60
A Shrub Palette 65
Plant Portrait: Early Camellias 68
Plant Portrait: Not Your Ordinary Azalea 70
A Few More Plants for the Shade 72
Hedges, Fences, and Walls 73
Don't Forget Vines 74
Trees 76
Plant Portrait: Fossil Fall Color 80

FLOWER BEDS AND BORDERS
82
The Center of Attention 85
The Big Bed 86
How Big Is Big Enough? 88
Think of Foliage First, But Begin with Roses 89
Thank Goodness for Perennials 91
Plant Portrait: The Dainty Dianthus 92
Garden Visit: One Big Border 94
Division and Dormancy 97

Garden Visit: Grandstand Gardening 98
A Place for Annuals 100
Plant Portrait: Pansies in Particular 103
A Place for Bulbs 108
Plant Portrait: Tricks with Tulips 109
Plant Portrait: More Bulb Stories 112
What About Wildflowers? 115
Garden Visit: A Wildflower Success Story 118

COLOR, HARMONY, AND CONTRAST
120
Simple Schemes 123
Hot, Cool, and True Blue 124
White, Gray, and Green 124
Plant Portrait: A Portfolio of White
Flowers 128
Plant Portrait: A Portfolio of Gray
Foliage 130
Plant Portrait: A Portfolio of Green
Flowers 134

DETAILS MAKE THE DIFFERENCE
136
Those Little Places 138
Accessories for the Garden 138
Garden Visit: A Compact City Garden with
Brilliant Touches 140
Plant Portrait: Plants Between
Paving Stones 142
A Place for Pots 144
Garden Visit: Paradise at Parklabrea 146
Water in the Garden 149
A Place for Good Tastes 150
A Kitchen Garden 153

PLANTING THE GARDEN
158
The Importance of Soil Preparation 160
Preparing a Garden Bed 162
Stomp It Down, Water, and Watch Out for
Weeds 164
Digging a Hole and Other Pertinent Planting
Information 166
Watering Wisdom, Staking, and
Mulching 168
The Zigs and Zags of Gardening 171

INDEX
172

PICTURE CREDITS
176

CHAPTER

1

WHAT
MAKES A
GARDEN?

The foyer for the secret garden is just inside the gate. Succulents grow in soil held in place by a layer of sphagnum moss inside a frame covered with chicken wire. They hang like a painting against the pink walls that protect the garden from the street. To the right of the gate is the entrance to the secret garden. The "secret" itself is the small enclosed garden built around a reflecting pool, pictured on pages 8 and 9.

THE POSSIBILITIES

The objective of this book is to explain the mystery that is the planning and planting of a garden—to show that it is really no mystery at all. There are certain rules and procedures that guide the process, and while with practice they can become quite sophisticated, they are basically simple.

The problem is that these rules are seldom remarked upon, or perhaps good and experienced gardeners are not even aware of the rules they are following, having naturally adopted certain procedures in the course of making a garden.

My hope is to speed up the process a little and help the reader avoid a lot of trial and error in making a garden. Having built a few gardens of my own, and having seen hundreds more, I have noticed that all good gardens follow similar principles, and I have attempted to organize these observations into the sections making up this book.

There are also special sections—Garden Visits and Plant Portraits—that show both the results of putting these rules into practice and some particular plants that work well.

Quite frankly, I wish I could have learned this information a little earlier in my own gardening career. It would have saved a lot of casting about—and a lot of work. There are more than a few plants in my garden that also might wish that I had discovered these rules a little sooner; many had to go because they were the wrong plant or in the wrong place.

At the very beginning I must add that results are not guaranteed—that is not in the nature of gardens and gardening. It would not be such a lively exercise and art if gardens could so easily be made perfect. Intrinsically,

they are living, growing things—quite different from the oils on an artist's canvas or the furniture in the house.

The kind of garden I have in mind is not cluttered with things. The garden I am thinking of is a simple but extremely satisfying place, devoted to plants and the experience of being outdoors, and a person's enjoyment of both. Only that person can finally plan such a garden.

If you are such a person, you should do the planting as well as the planning so you know what is going on in your garden. Planting something, then watching it grow in a richly prepared soil of your own concoction is the basic charm of gardening. Framing the plant or tree or shrub so it sits in the garden like a sparkling jewel in an exquisite setting is the challenge of planning, or garden design.

Perhaps the hardest part of planning a garden is simply recognizing all the possibilities. There are so many, yet they are so seldom fully employed. Here we have a whole box of crayons to play with, but when it comes time to begin the planning, we take out only the black. What crayons never got out of the box?

The purpose of this book is also to look at some of the possibilities in a garden—the play of light, the warmth of the sun, the sense of surprise, the drama that is possible. These ingredients are often overlooked perhaps because, as adults, we are wary of making mistakes and prefer the safe approach. Given a big box of crayons, most of us would stick to the safe colors, while a child wouldn't hesitate to use every crayon in the box. Neither should we. And if there is one absolute rule in gardening it is that almost everything takes its own time. The best plants grow slowly, and so do the best plans.

Garden Visit

THE SECRET GARDEN

The centerpiece of this garden in Santa Monica is a secret. It cannot be seen from the street, even though it is in front of the house and abuts the sidewalk. You do not get to it in a direct line, but must work your way up a wide walk into a small courtyard and through narrow passageways. You may not even see it until you are inside the house since the entrance to this secret garden is situated obliquely. But along the way you will discover some of the possibilities inherent in a garden.

The entry walk (page 15) only hints at what is to come. It is wide, expansive, and wonderfully planted. The designer, Nancy Goslee Power, sees it as a transitional space. She believes in "good, generous entrances" and favors a straight line to the door, or in this

case to the front gate. There is no
leisurely curve or tricky paving to trip
you up, but this is not a boulevard
either. Mounding, chaparral-like
plants (but from other Mediterranean
climates), including a huge silvery licorice plant, *Helichrysum petiolatum*,
and billowy lavender, creep onto the
paving, softening the severity of a
straight path.

The colors of the walk, walls, and
gate in front of you are muted and
earthy but colorful nonetheless. These
are not "grayed" but "umbered"
colors, a touch of that muddy brown
pigment having been added to the
paint. The plants are gray and
glaucous green, the flowers subtle, and
the foliage scented. Even the normally
boisterous bougainvillea that covers
the entry area is a soft, pale pinkish-
white variety. Inside the gate the colors become a shade brighter until they
reach a burnt-orange bougainvillea
draped over the front door. This is
'Orange King,' which in time will mix
with a bougainvillea named 'California
Gold' still struggling to grow out of
the shadow of the house.

In the center of this inner courtyard,
tucked into the space left by the
L-shaped house, is a Spanish-style pool
in keeping with the architecture. It is
kept full to the brim, a perfect mirror
for the bougainvillea that you see as
you enter or for the huge chimney
above the outdoor fireplace at the left.
The pool, so full and wet it has water
on its rim and puddles at its feet,
makes the courtyard feel cool on hot
days, while the fireplace, aglow after
sundown, warms those chilly coastal
nights. The courtyard was designed to
be the center of the house—a true
outdoor room—since the house is
quite small.

But, wait, you've walked right past
the entrance to the secret garden. You

Just past the entry garden and foyer is this secluded patio, with a fireplace to warm the chilly Santa Monica nights, and a small pool filled to overflowing to cool the warm summer days. A bougainvillea named 'Orange King' spills from the veranda roof and a climbing rose named 'Mermaid' covers the wall. They are the wallpaper in this outdoor room.

Ordinary Palos Verdes stone is used elegantly for the steps and walls that were laid up dry without mortar. Alchemilla pectinata, *with its crinkled foliage, creeps through the cracks. The cloud of pink flowers belongs to a Mexican evening primrose.*

Separating the inner patio from the street is this wall, nearly obscured by luxuriant plantings of a dark purple lavender, the gray stems and white flowers of a lychnis, and tiny white Santa Barbara daisies. A variegated New Zealand flax stands guard at the gate.

can see it through a little window in the courtyard wall, so you know it's there, but you must back up a few feet and go through the gate just to the left of the entrance gate to get to it. When one gate is open, the other is hidden; that's how you missed it.

Now you come out under a stunning subtropical shrub with smoky purple flowers, *Iochroma cyaneum,* and, surprise, this garden is sunken as well as secret. This is one reason you do not notice it from the street, for it is actually lower than the sidewalk, even though the house is considerably higher. That garden is so low that the pool in the bottom does not drain but floods the sunken section. When this

happens (after a hard rain), the fish sneak out and nibble at the plants growing between the paving stones, and then retreat back to their pool when the water eventually recedes and soaks into the soil.

The front yard remained unimproved for quite a while until the idea of sinking it came to Nancy Power. It promised to liven up a potentially monotonous area that is quite small and was as flat as the proverbial pancake. The garden could have felt cramped because of the hedges surrounding it, but sinking it changed "cramped" to "cozy."

"It doesn't take much—step down two feet and it is surprising how dif-

ferent the space feels," observes Power. "You forget where it is (right next to the street) and the whole sense of scale changes."

The retaining wall is of Palos Verdes stone, often undistinguished, but looking surprisingly fine in this garden, perhaps because of the way the wall is built. It is laid up dry, without mortar, and steps back steeply. Despite lectures by masons to the effect that this is not how to build a wall, Power insisted it be done this way, pointing out drawings in a Gertrude Jekyll folio showing fine English walls. The wall works admirably at holding the soil in place and, as a bonus, makes a stage or perch for some of her favorite plants.

Because this is her own garden, Power broke one of her strict planting design rules—never use just one plant. Other designers call it "the rule of three's and five's," believing that three or five of anything looks better than one. But here "there are lots of one's," Power confesses.

This secret garden is, in fact, a plant person's paradise, chock-full of fascinating candidates for a garden. The most subtle of these, and one of Power's better discoveries on a nursery-shopping adventure, was found at the elegant Western Hills Nursery in Northern California. It's an *Alchemilla,* which has rooted into the mortarless joints of the wall next to the steps

leading into the garden, with exquisitely crinkled leaves and coloring a near match for the stone. This is the way much of the garden holds itself together—colors are controlled and build on a theme.

The inspiration for a secret garden came from the children's classic of the same name by Frances Hodgson Burnett, and the idea of creating one was hatched during a stay in England. The primary purpose was to improve the view from the house. As in many houses of this style and vintage, the largest window looked out onto the street, which wasn't much of a view. Now that window frames the secret garden and its still, moss-green pool.

A garden notebook should be the beginning of your garden as well as its permanent record. Anything that might help with the planning or planting should be included so it can be quickly found. In the author's own notebook, dried flowers and a photograph are reminders of a favorite color scheme. Rather than draw plans, build a three-dimensional model like the one shown here. These walls are made of foam-core, readily available at art supply stores. A scale ruler is a big help when making models or drawing plans.

WHERE TO BEGIN: THE NOTEBOOK

So, where does one begin to plan a garden? On paper, by taking note of what you have, what you would like, and what you may have seen somewhere else that pleases you.

These notes will be the beginning of a garden notebook, scrapbook, and diary that will direct your efforts. Most good gardeners keep one, and some have turned into literature, but what you want to accumulate are ideas, not just words. Take snapshots of the garden as it looks now, from vantage points that are important to you and your life—out the kitchen window for instance. Take photographs of plants you admire in other gardens, or in botanic gardens, and make a note of when they are in flower and how large they are (an important consideration as we'll see later). If you don't know what the plant is, you can show the photographs to a nurseryman later when it's time to purchase these furnishings for the garden.

When you see a picture of a garden you like in a magazine, cut the photograph out and paste it in this notebook; make notes of garden pictures seen in books, or photocopy the pages. Samples of wood stains, paving, and pieces of gravel can also find their way into your files. In fact, it is a good idea to start a little collection of these man-made things in some corner of the garden so you can refer to them and live with them for a while, to see if the color or texture is as pleasing as you first thought.

Live With It Living with it for a while is a very important part of planning your garden. Many expert designers suggest that you first live in a garden for at least a year so you can observe the seasons change and can discover where the most important parts of the garden for you actually are.

If you simply can't wait to get started, garden for a year with annuals and other short-lived plants. This will give you a feel for the weather and the soil, but you won't be committed to any long-term projects. I can guarantee that after living in a garden for a year you will feel differently about it.

Plans Are for the Birds What you do not want to do is draw plans on paper. Plans are only two-dimensional, and a case can be made that gardens have become a lot less interesting since professional designers started drawing plans. Most of the world's great gardens were never planned on paper. Their designers conceived them by walking about and deciding where in the earth this or that should go. Plans drawn on paper show a design that only the birds can see, from above. Instead, keep your feet on the ground and learn to envision a garden from ground level, as you might see it when walking through it.

Gardens are three-dimensional creations, but put them on a flat piece of paper and that all-important third dimension is lost. How can you tell on a plan if a tree is so low it must be ducked under, or if a shrub is tall enough to hide something? You want to be able to get a sense of what being in the garden is actually like, but you can't experience it on a paper plan.

For example, paths that are fun to follow often look awkward from a bird's view; they can only be designed by laying them out on the ground and then trying them out. Because of perspective, even formal paths that are as straight as an arrow look very different on the ground than on a plan. On the ground, the lines seem to converge in the distance; they do not on a plan.

Make a Model Instead If you want to test your ideas before you actually begin the work, try building a model of the garden. Use scraps of cardboard or the much fancier foam-core board used by architects. Make a base, complete with slope if your garden is on rolling terrain, then add the fences and the walls of the house. Be sure to put doors and windows in your walls so you can actually look out onto the garden from inside your model house. Foam-core (available at art supply stores) is especially easy to work with because it can be cut quickly with a single-edged razor blade and a steel rule, is rigid enough to stand on its own, and can be glued in a snap with ordinary white glue. Cardboard is cheaper (use an old box) but is hard to cut and glue.

You will find this model very helpful because it takes much less imagination to see what the garden will look like in three dimensions. You can make little trees and bushes and move them around until they create a vista you like. You can even plant little beds of flowers and, more than that, you can take this model outdoors and see just what will be in shade and what will be in sun at various times of the year.

Plans on paper do have their use, but they should be the last thing you do. They are, in effect, a big notepad that you can refer to during construction, covered with important dimensions and names of plants. But your master plan had better be a model.

CLIMATE AND LOCATION

Location determines what can be grown in a garden and what creature comforts may be necessary. Most people are aware of their climate—is it hot or cold, or both, or not especially either—but they may not be aware of what can be grown in their climate. Though part of the fun of gardening is trying to do what oughtn't to be possible, these adventures should be the exception and, in general, a garden should reflect its climate. The United States Department of Agriculture pub-

A. *On a hillside a fence or wall acts like a dam, trapping cold air behind it.*

B. *Cold air rolls off a roof, while plants tucked under the eaves are protected.*

C. *The north side of the house is always cool and shady; the south side hot and sunny. There are plants that will be happiest in either extreme.*

D. *Cold air runs down hills and collects in valley bottoms; thus hillsides are often warmer than valleys in winter and may be considered "banana belts."*

A.

B.

C.

D.

lishes a map that divides the country into ten climate zones, which take into account how cold it gets in winter. But the heat of summer is just as limiting a factor, as is the amount of moisture in the air. This information is not as readily available.

In California, the climate is complex enough to have prompted the state to further subdivide this unique area into twenty-four distinct climatic zones, from seashore to mountaintop to desert. California gardeners can find these zones listed on the excellent maps in the *Sunset Western Garden Book,* and in this dictionary of gardening the description of each plant includes a note indicating in which of these zones it does best.

Take Notes on Your Garden's Climate
Your garden notebook can help if you begin to write down what you observe about your climate, and what you hear from others on the subject. Gardeners, more than most people, like to talk about the weather and its peculiarities. There are a few things in particular to look for. Gardens contain microclimates that can affect plant and human happiness. Cold air tends to settle, to flow to the lowest point. It behaves much like water and can even become entrapped behind a wall. Atriums, surrounded on all four sides by walls, tend to become filled with cold air much like a bathtub with water. Fences that are built too solid dam cold air moving down a slope. Eaves on a house and trees with overhanging branches tend to protect plants from cold by insulating them from the sky.

Plants close to the ground are most likely to be blackened by frost because cold air collects near the ground. This is why small tender saplings are more likely to succumb to winter cold than taller, older trees.

Microclimates Look for pockets of warmth or cold early in the morning and in the middle of the day, and on a rough plan of your garden make a note of their location. In this way, you may find the perfect place for a certain plant that needs more or less warmth. Or you may find the places to avoid. You may also discover the spot in all your garden that you would most enjoy —the future home of a patio or deck.

Perhaps the most obvious differences, or microclimates, in a garden are the north and south sides of a house, the one being cold even in summer, the other hot. Many gardeners have observed that some plants will grow in such a cool or warm spot, whereas they will not grow out in the garden, away from the house. Citrus, for example, needs extra warmth, camellias need a little extra coolness or shade.

This north-south difference is also marked on sloping ground, the north side of a hill being much cooler than the south. In California, this is apparent because most of the trees and shrubs tend to grow on north-facing slopes, while south-facing slopes tend to have grasses or the toughest of shrubs that can withstand the hot, dry summer sun.

Banana Belts Be aware that gardens planted on the sides of hills are in an environment drained of cold air and therefore they experience milder winter temperatures. These hillsides are often called "banana belts" because they are just enough warmer to grow tender plants, though maybe not warm enough actually to grow bananas. The cold air flows down to the valley bottoms, where it collects. In Southern California, valleys became the home of deciduous fruit-tree orchards that needed more winter cold, while citrus and avocados that thrive in warm, dry climates took to the hillsides.

Breezes, Santa Anas, and Other Seasonal Winds Wind also plays a part in the garden's location and should be taken into account. Prevailing winds that cool a garden and help circulate the air should be encouraged to enter. Do not inadvertently block these with tall plantings or solid walls. Good air movement in a garden is surprisingly important to the health of plants—as well as to the comfort of people. Still air fosters plant diseases, while breezes discourage them. For this reason it is often difficult to grow things in small or enclosed places, or in corners. Plants particularly susceptible to disease, such as roses, should be out in the open where air circulates freely, in the best of light.

Ferocious seasonal winds, such as Southern California's notorious Santa Ana or devil wind, are another matter and should be excluded from the garden as much as possible by plantings or structures. Typically, these winds come from an entirely different direction than is normal. In the case of a Santa Ana, the wind comes from the north or east, while the prevailing wind is from the west. So plan your walls and tall plantings accordingly.

LIGHT

Light is perhaps the most important influence on a garden, not just because it is so necessary for plant growth, but because the garden's very appearance depends upon it. Think of these various kinds of light and how different the mood is of each:

The soft morning sun, skimming low across the garden, distinctly rosy colored as it adds a pink highlight to just the tips of plants.

The warm glow of the late afternoon sun that turns even pink flowers a shade of orange.

The cool, colorless light of an overcast day, or the dark gray-blue light just before rain.

The midday summer sun that makes almost no shadows and bleaches all but the brightest colors.

Each of these lighting conditions is remarkably different and each will give the garden a remarkably different look, even if nothing else changed. If no leaves fell in winter and no flowers bloomed in spring, you could probably tell by the light what time of year it was, and what time of day. If you think these are givens and not something to remember when planning a garden, consider these points:

Flower beds can be designed to catch either the morning or the afternoon light, whichever is your favorite or coincides with your time at home and out in the garden.

Pink and blue flowers seem to glow on overcast days, but are almost invisible in the bright light of noon on a clear summer's day; yellow and orange blooms, on the other hand, look their best on a sunny day when the sun is high overhead, but look oddly out of place on a cool, cloudy day.

There is almost no point planting pink or blue flowers for midsummer, when they will not show to advantage. Perhaps that is why so many bloom in spring, when the light is low and cool and days overcast, so they can look their best.

Summer's flowers naturally tend toward yellow or orange, taking full advantage of that bright yellow sun and deep blue sky.

Most discoveries about garden light

Tulips especially, but also ranunculus, love to grow in just a smattering of shade, as do these plantings beneath the birch trees. Bare in winter when the spring bulbs are growing, the trees leaf out just as the bulbs come into bloom, protecting them from a spring sun that sometimes becomes too hot. In summer, when the bulbs are dormant, the fully leafed out birches keep them cool.

are made by accident—you happen to notice that something you planted looks great right now because the sun is where it is. Make a note about which plants look best in each lighting situation. Some flowers are prettiest when lit from above, but many more take on a special glow when lit from behind or from the side. Write down which look especially dramatic with the sun coming through the petals or which look extra rich in the ruddy light of a setting sun. If you are on an early morning walk and notice that the Iceland poppies in a neighbor's yard look wonderfully dramatic because the low sun is lighting every petal as if it were a piece of stained glass, make a note of this, and next time, plant your poppies to stand between you and the morning sun.

Look for pools of sun that might spotlight certain plants; try some beds facing east, some west, and some south. A variety of lighting situations will make the garden change throughout the day and throughout the year, as stage lighting can make changes in the same scene.

Painters and photographers have noticed that the light in various parts of the world can be remarkably different, and gardeners who have toted their cameras along on garden tours to other climates have probably seen the same thing. Using the same film and techniques employed at home often results in poor garden photographs when the light is different. To make your garden look its best, take advantage of your climate's unique light.

SHADOWS AND SHADE

If at all possible, one does not want to garden in the shade. Most plants do not like it, though some may tolerate it. There are enough challenges in gardening without taking on this one.

There are degrees of shadow—the deep shade under a big, dense tree may make it impossible for plants to grow, but the dappled shade found under a tree with a more open canopy may be just right. Many bulbs seem to do best in the lightest of shade, and many flowers (even roses) exhibited at shows are grown in some shade. It makes the colors brighter and the flowers larger, though the plants may produce fewer flowers and they will certainly grow taller and looser, their stems floppier, and leaves spaced further apart.

In general, however, most plants crave all the sun they can get, while people would just as soon stay out of it. This suggests that it might be better to put your patio in the shade of a tree or house, and leave the sunny spots for plants. Very shady places are also good for a toolshed, a woodpile, or anything that does not need sun to grow.

A Shade Map Before going much further with your planning, you should map the shadows in your garden, so you know precisely where they fall. This is easily done during one sunny day. On a rough drawing of your garden, color the areas that are in shadow at about 10 A.M., then with a different colored pencil at noon, and again, with yet another color at 3 P.M. You will now see clearly where the sunniest spots in the garden are (they will not be colored at all on your plan) and where the shadiest places are (they will have the most colors).

Lengthening Shadows You may want to make a map for summer and one for winter because the sun does not stay in the same place. In Southern California, in the middle of summer, the sun is 79 degrees above the horizon at high

While most plants don't like to grow in shade, a few thrive if the shade does not become too dark. The avocado is one of the most difficult trees to garden under, but prune some lower branches, thus raising the canopy, and enough light sneaks through for impatiens. Shady areas are also good choices for paving and places to sit.

SHADE MAP

A. *Drawing lines with colored pencils, map the shadows in your garden at different times of the day so you know which areas are shady and which are not. Here we see the shadows at 10 a.m., noon, and 3 p.m. Where the lines overlap most densely there will be deepest shade, the most difficult places to grow things in the garden.*

B. *In summer, when the sun is high, shadows fall directly beneath the object casting them.*

C. *In winter the shadows lengthen and an object may cast its shadow well out in the garden; but the sun also slants under the object—a tree in this case—so normally shaded areas are suddenly in sunlight, though it is the weak sun of winter. It's a good idea to make a shade map for both winter and summer.*

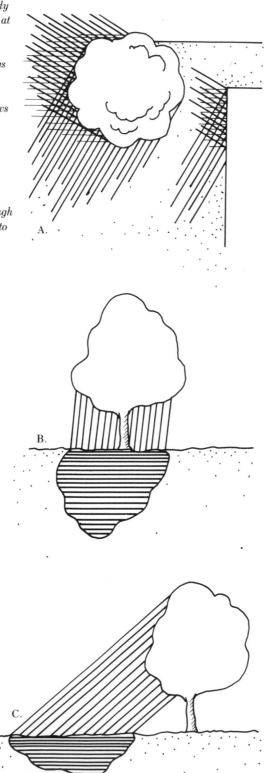

noon, nearly overhead; in winter, at the same time of day, it is only 33 degrees above the horizon, half as high in the sky. This means that shadows are more than six times longer in winter. Your house's shadow may only extend three feet into the garden in summer, but it stretches about eighteen feet in winter. Plants that grow in sun all summer are suddenly in shade all winter. This can pose a few problems for the gardener because most plants that can grow in the shade do not want suddenly to find themselves in the sun, and vice versa. You can avoid this drastic change of conditions by using plants that do their growing and flowering in summer, when they can be in full sun, and are dormant or resting in winter, when they will have to be in shadow.

Roses are dormant in winter, but by the time they begin to leaf out, the sun has climbed higher in the sky and they are in sunlight. *Pittosporum tobira* 'Wheeler's Dwarf' is a slightly different example: While it does not go dormant in winter, it only grows in late spring when the sun is high enough not to effect the new growth.

A Secret Spot The reverse occurs under trees or overhead structures such as a patio covering. Plants that grow in the shade, when the summer sun is high overhead, are bathed in soft light all winter as the sun sneaks under the canopy of foliage or the patio roof. In fact, a favorite place for tulips is under the very edge of a tree's leafy canopy. They grow in the sun during winter and spring, but flower in increasing shade, which helps the flowers last longer and bloom more brightly. When this area is completely shaded in summer, the tulips are finished, and their place is taken by plants that can grow in shade. Impatiens often are volunteers for the job.

CHAPTER

2

FROM
THE GROUND
UP

Paths are absolutely essential to the design of a garden; they define its very style. The path on page 27 sets a casual, informal tone for its garden and begs for further exploration. What's around the corner? The bright golden coreopsis is a focal point when in flower, while a comfortable garden bench is inviting at all seasons.

In this chapter, you will also discover some intriguing alternatives to a lawn, such as the checkerboard hedge on pages 24–25. It provides open space (and considerable interest) in a small, urban garden. The gray squares are Santolina chamaecyparissus and the green S. virens.

THE IMPORTANCE OF PATHS

The paths through a garden are too often an afterthought, when they should be considered first. But before we plan our paths, let's start fresh. Try to block out all previous ideas of what a path should or should not be. Do not see a path as a narrow band of concrete that gets you to the front door or down the side yard. Do not see the lawn as a path. True, it gets you almost anywhere in the garden, but you are going to get your feet wet or muddy walking across it, the wheelbarrow is going to bog down, and, more to the point, the lawn lacks any direction or focus so the eye tends to wander nervously looking for something to settle on.

Try instead to see a path as "the tracks the eye rides upon," as Hugh Johnson has so neatly put it, because this is precisely what a path does more than anything else—it guides the eye through the garden as if it were riding on steel rails, and only later do the feet follow. Paths certainly have their utilitarian purposes, but in most gardens it isn't too important if they lead you somewhere or not because you can't wander very far afield on the average piece of property. The important thing is that a path must appear to lead somewhere. And, the further away it seems to lead, the better.

In garden design, the shortest distance between two points is not always the best place for a path. It is better to draw out the experience, to prolong that all-too-short journey through the garden, which, while you're taking it, makes the garden seem much larger than it is, satisfying a craving shared by nearly every gardener for a little more acreage. Japanese gardens often contain tortuous paths—they seem designed to trip you up—but no one really wants you to fall on your face,

just slow down and notice what is around you.

While a path can twist and turn in its routing, it should not be too narrow. In fact, a path can never be too wide. A four-foot-wide path is about the minimum. It will barely accommodate two people walking side-by-side—or a wheelbarrow. Visually, anything narrower makes a garden seem cramped and the gardener a little stingy with his paving materials. Paths give a garden focus and structure. A strong path tells you where to look, and along the way you discover the other parts of a garden. First, decide where the path is to go, and the other elements of a garden will begin to fall into place.

Formal or Informal? It could be said that a formal path makes a formal garden, an informal path, an informal garden. A formal garden is one that looks distinctly man-made, where most of the lines are straight; an informal plan is more natural in appearance, with most of the lines curved, though it may be just as contrived. Classical gardens were formal in plan until the eighteenth century, when the English began making them more natural in appearance. Formal gardens did not disappear overnight, and they are still very much with us. But from the late eighteenth century until today, most gardens have depended on curving lines and curving paths to achieve a natural look.

In today's small, enclosed gardens, where no distant view or vista is available, formal plans once again make a great deal of sense. Where the garden area is almost roomlike, a rectilinear arrangement of the spaces—paths, flower beds, patios—looks less contrived than a plan that seeks to imitate nature, which is seldom forced to work on such a small canvas. In a formal

A formal path needs a focal point at its destination. At the end of this ample path of decomposed granite (better known as "d.g."), ivy spilling from an antique urn makes an elegant center of attention. Note how this path's thoroughly compacted, gritty soil is mounded, the better to shed water.

A distant pool of light is the focal point for the formal brick path on page 29, beckoning one to explore further. Foxgloves and dainty coral bells line the way.

garden plan, one path dominates the scene and leads somewhere within sight. It might run from the back door to the back fence, in a straight line, and at its end is a distinct focal point. In classical gardens, this was often a statue or fountain, and these are still good candidates for the job. Whatever the focal point, it must stand out from its surroundings.

A Focal Point for a Formal Garden In a smallish garden, the focal point is very important and some time should be spent to find just the perfect object. It should be complicated enough so that every detail is not visible from the other end of the path—you want visitors to come out into the garden curious to see just what this thing is. In my own garden I used a very large pot

The formal and informal garden plans on this page illustrate in a nutshell how the key differences are determined by the paths. One curves and disappears around a corner, the other is straight and focused, in this case, on a small fountain set off to one side.

In a turnabout from conventional planning, the spa and pool on page 31 were pushed into a corner and the rose garden was planted next to the house. The plan for this garden is classically formal—paths are at right angles and as straight as arrows.

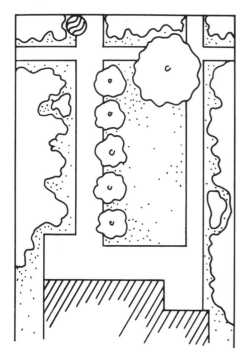

A FORMAL PLAN

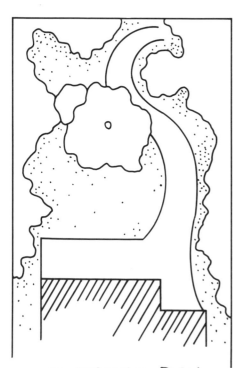

AN INFORMAL PLAN

filled with water, fish, and aquatic plants. The container is simple enough to stand out from its surroundings without being an obvious eyesore, and the plants and fish are of sufficient interest to coax even nongardeners to go and see what's blooming or how the fish are faring. Visitors are always drawn to the far end of the garden.

In large formal gardens, the focal point is often the distant horizon. The focal point at Vaux-le-Vicomte—the most famous formal French garden that led Louis XIV to appropriate the landscape designer André Le Nôtre for his own gardens at Versailles—is a perfectly proportioned opening in the trees framing the vista of a distant hill. A later owner added a huge statue of Hercules, which overstates the point.

In a plan for a formal garden, there may be other paths leading off in other directions; the main path may be set anywhere in the garden (even running from one side to the other if that is the longest dimension and main axis of the garden), but that path should be the first thing the visitor discovers so it can immediately organize the garden for the eye. There should be no doubt where to look and at what.

No End in Sight In an informal plan, the path should not have an obvious end, any more than a trail through the woods has an obvious end. It should appear to go on and on and simply disappear around a corner, with no end in sight. The object of our attention at the end of an informal path is not so much a focal point as a vanishing point—we are attracted to that point when our view is obscured. Like a trail through the woods, this path must also make some sense. There must be a reason for those curves, something that is overlooked in many plans for an informal garden. On a trail, curves

exist so the trail can go around trees or boulders, or follow contours of the land.

In gardens, paths often curve for no reason, and they end up looking quite unnatural because there is no organic purpose for their behavior, and the ever-questioning mind wonders—even unconsciously—"why do these paths wander all over the place?" It is easy enough to invent some *raison d'être* for this meandering: Mound up the soil in the beds that border the path so it seems to be following the low ground, as a stream will do; or place boulders in the way, so it must curve around them, or trees, or a mass of flowers.

To make a path without end requires some space, so formal plans are perhaps to be favored in tight places, though it is possible to fool the eye that your meandering path goes on and on. Simply let it curve around a corner or some tall shrubs, and out of sight. Hide its end and few will be the wiser.

The Draw Both kinds of path tend to draw one out into the garden—the formal plan has that fascinating object at its end, urging one to investigate, and the informal plan teases one into trying to discover what's around the corner—precisely what you want and one good reason for a strong path. Visit a garden that has only a large lawn area in back, and no distinct path, and most people end up standing by the back door, never venturing further. Visit a garden with a bold path, and most people spend only seconds by the back door before heading off on their adventure through the garden. Of course, there is much more to garden design, but a strong path is a great start. Once it has drawn you into the garden, you must make sure that something else is out there that makes the trip worthwhile. And that is the rest of garden design.

Garden Visit

A FORMAL PLAN FOR ROSES

One could say that roses have not been treated right by us gardeners. In recent years they have been relegated to their own barren corner of the yard, like royalty in exile. Though rose bushes have the grandest flowers and bloom most of the year, though they have colors more vibrant and varied than other flowers, and though they have not fallen from popularity in the least, they are most often forced to grow alone—away from the other lovely lords and ladies of the garden—in the humblest of surroundings. There they are kept for cutting, while the hoi polloi of marigolds and the like are planted in the best places. Never mind that the gardener might lavish attention on his roses, planting them with great care, pruning and primping them in the proper season, and pam-

pering them in general—they deserve to be given pride of place. And lately there are a few rose fanciers who are seeking to do just that.

Landscape architect Mark Berry of Pasadena and Aptos, California, was fortunate enough to find one such rose fancier as a client, fortunate because the client sought a formal solution to the problem of where to put roses, and Berry favors formal gardens. This formal garden is small, located behind a typical ranch-style house. The garden boasts a delightful collection of thirty-four rose bushes, and they are not crowded together in a corner of the yard. Instead, the swimming pool that the client also fancied was put in the corner, so what you see from the living room windows is a garden of roses.

The garden is still quite young in these photographs but that points out a seldom-considered benefit of a formal

To soften the hard edges of the paths in the garden below, the designer used the delicate shapes of star jasmine for the low hedges that form the borders. At path's end (just out of camera range) a bench attracts the eye.

The informal garden at the right has nary a hard edge in sight. The path curves around the house and disappears, but it is enticing and the wisteria-covered arch at the end only makes it more so. To the left of the path are a mix of tall cannas, statice, salvia, and annual phlox.

plan: The straight lines and precise edges give formal gardens a finished look right from the start, even before the plants grow up or the hedges fill in.

The plan is as linear as you can get, and it has the opposite effect of what one might expect—it makes the garden look larger than life. At the end of the major path is a humble garden

bench, which serves well as an inviting focal point. To add some complexity and interest, benches are set in little alcoves along the paths. The garden is surrounded by tall leafy shrubs that screen out neighboring yards and is crisscrossed with low hedges of star jasmine. Berry likes the jasmine hedges because they are a gentle, billowy contrast to the very linear, rigid

paths; and he points out that, though the plan is very sharp and formal, the materials are all soft, even the paving —a 3½-inch-deep layer of decomposed granite. The low hedges have another benefit: while the tops of rose bushes are something to admire, the bottoms beg to be hidden, which the hedges do admirably. Hedges might be considered formal attire for roses.

Garden Visit

AN INFORMAL PLAN

Gardens are often called living canvasses upon which the gardener paints with plants. If that is so, most of us are content with fairly simple compositions—a few bold strokes of color against a background of uniform green—simple but satisfying, until one sees what are the other possibilities.

Here, for instance, is a garden sure to inspire greater flights of horticultural fancy. This is the Poway, California, garden of professional illustrator Karen Kees, who increasingly spends time away from her paints and palette, devoting it instead to garden design. The artist shows in the fearless, almost brazen, combinations of colors that one might not expect to make such good companions—such as pink with orange—and in the sheer exuberance of it all. The Kees garden is also an excellent example of an informal plan. The paths go nowhere in particular,

but they enticingly disappear around corners so you can't help but follow them. At the far end of one path is an additional tease, a tipsy trellis smothered with vines that looks like a gateway into yet another, surely wonderful, part of the garden, though actually the garden doesn't extend much further.

This is, in fact, an average-size yard in the middle of a housing tract; it's not as rural as it appears. The walls and roofs in the background belong to other houses, but most of that view is screened by dense plantings so you are hardly aware of the neighbors' existence. And the foreground is so convincingly rustic that you don't question its location in the country. The paths are gravel with stones and boulders that look as though they have been washed up along its sides, suggesting a stream-bed rather than a garden path.

Everywhere the plants threaten to overgrow, if not overwhelm, the garden. They creep onto the paths, sometimes growing right in the middle of them, climb every wall, scamper across the roof, and reach for the sky. The reason you can't see around the corners, and the reason the paths wander, is that they are following the low ground between mounds of soil, which also provide excellent drainage for the flowers and a platform so they are better viewed. If the plants look richly satisfied, it has to do with the soil preparation: The beds are half organic amendment and half soil, a luxurious mix for a luxuriant paint-box planting.

PAVING POSSIBILITIES

Probably no other material used in a garden is as important as the paving you walk on, because it is so visually dominating. The texture and color establishes a look for the garden—a rough texture and earthy colors make the garden appear natural; smooth textures and brighter colors indicate that the garden is man-made. The best way to choose a paving material is to buy some samples and leave them lying about in the garden while you continue your planning. Generally, the best paving is not laid as a solid mass but is made up of individual pieces, such as bricks, large tiles, and stepping stones. Don't overlook compacted earth as a paving material, such as the decomposed granite used a lot in California, and do be aware that the glare of the sun off some materials (concrete in particular) can be bothersome.

A good method of paving is to put the material on top of a base of sand, with sand filling the gaps between pavers so rain can run through to the

Where does an informal path go? The idea is not to let anyone find out—it should appear to go on forever. Here it flows like a dry stream through a bed of daylilies and a wild mix of flowers. Gravel makes an appropriate paving.

Even the decidedly rectangular shape of common bricks can make an informal path, like the meandering beauty on this page. This classic paving pattern flows through the garden. The bricks are laid on sand and plants grow in the cracks, further softening the composition.

Grass is not always the appropriate choice, aesthetically or environmentally, for covering ground. On a sunny hillside in the Santa Monica Mountains, two pads of decomposed granite provide open space and a warm, dry place to sun. The strong row of Italian cypress in the background adds to the Mediterranean mood.

When drought-resistant plantings are called for, something other than lawn grasses must be used. In the garden on page 37 a combination of gravel and tiles was successfully employed. Sedum spectabile is the pink-flowered accent.

roots, which are inevitably underneath. Should those roots begin to lift the paving, or should the ground settle, individual pavers set on sand will not crack or break, and they can be lifted up and relaid.

LAWNS, PATIOS, AND OTHER OPEN SPACES

When you have mentally laid out your paths—and perhaps plotted them on paper—it is time to think about the other low, open spaces in the garden, the meadows, if you will, that border our trail through the woods. I like this analogy because it helps put lawns, and even patios, in perspective. So often lawns are laid down as if they were carpeting, from wall to wall. But if you think of them as meadow areas, they become much more flexible. They can then be large or small, long, narrow, or wide-spreading, regular or

irregular in shape. They don't have to be contiguous but can be scattered through the garden like the little glades discovered on a hike through the woods.

Your Personal Park Lawns are open areas, which keep a space from feeling cramped, personal parks, or meadows that can be walked on, played on, laid on. They take surprisingly little care; weeds that invade get mowed along with the grass and become part of the lawn. Dead patches are easily replaced and the entire lawn can be watered automatically without a great deal of precision—too much or too little water is not likely to be fatal, as it is with so many other plants. A really good lawn, green, healthy, and weed-free, is no small achievement, but if you are willing to settle for something less than perfection, as are most gardeners, there is nothing as easy to grow as a lawn. Without a doubt, that is why they cover such a large part of so many gardens.

A Real Luxury Some gardeners feel that there is nothing quite as elegant as a rich green carpet of grass. Landscape architect Bill Evans, who designed several of the Disney theme parks and who has a passion for plants, concedes: "One of the real luxuries of garden design is a great sweep of lawn. There is just no substitute for lawn." People with children also know that a lawn saves wear and tear on the house, since children can do their roughhousing outdoors on the soft grass. A strong case could be made that lawns are a necessary part of any garden visited by children.

But are they the only option?

The Shrinking Lawn Lawns are the consummate consumers of water, and so they are coming under close scrutiny in many parts of the country where water must be husbanded. Thriftier lawn grasses are on the way. The thirstiest—bluegrass—is already being replaced by a group of deep-rooted grasses called tall fescues; and in the sunbelt Bermudagrass, St. Augustine, and hybrid zoysias are gaining popularity because they need so little water. New varieties of these subtropical grasses have a much shortened dormant season in winter and finer leaves.

But smaller areas of lawn are likely to replace the lavish spreads of grass in the near future just because styles and ideas about what makes a good garden are changing. Gardeners across the country are already busy digging out sections of lawn to make way for more flowers or vegetables. (Less lawn may even be mandated as some communities consider limiting how much of a garden can be planted to turf.)

Plans A and B For the last hundred years or so gardens have been designed around their lawns. First the largest lawn possible for your space was laid out, then the perimeter planted with flowers or shrubs, and then other features were added. Let's call this Plan A. If you now begin to see lawns as a smaller part of the landscape, or as no part of it at all, the whole balance of the garden begins to change. Let's call this Plan B, which begins with paths and then adds other open spaces. This is exactly how the newer gardens are designed: First the paths are decided on, then the areas on either side—some are lawns, but some are other kinds of paving, including patios.

Patios As far as the design of a garden is concerned, patios can be treated just

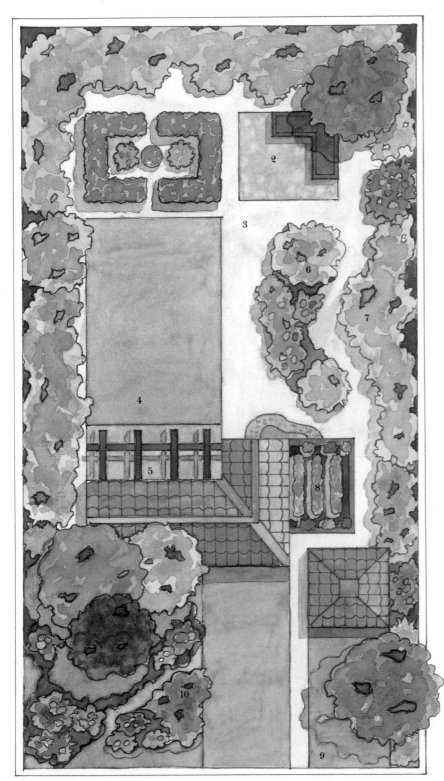

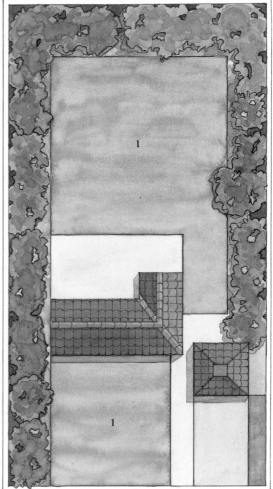

PLAN A

1. Lots of lawn

PLAN B

1. Water feature
2. Small, shaded patio
3. Decomposed granite paths
4. Smaller lawn
5. Smaller patio, now shaded
6. Flowers or ground-covering shrubs
7. Perimeter planting of drought-tolerant shrubs
8. Kitchen garden
9. Paving shaded by tree
10. Ground-covering shrubs

like lawns—they are still simply open spaces, with a harder surface. Patios are generally put right next to the house. They are handy there, functioning like an additional room, and they also help to catch some of the dirt that might get tracked into the house. Patios are often made quite large in the hope that they will be used for entertaining. But as any observer of parties can tell you, people like to congregate in smaller clusters, and when the party takes place in the house, some guests end up in the kitchen, some in the dining room, and only some remain in the living room (where they are all supposed to be).

When the party takes place outdoors, in the garden, the same holds true. So there is good reason to divide one large patio into several smaller, more intimate, areas, as shown in Plan B. When you are alone on one of these smaller patios, it is a cozy experience. And because there are several, each patio can have its own personality, allowing you to pick and choose where you would most like to sit.

No Lost Space Large expanses of paving are avoided in Plan B, but if you make each path wider and scatter several small patios through the garden, you will have the same amount of open, usable, outdoor space as you did with a lawn, while avoiding that parking lot look. Because paving can increase the amount of reflected heat in the garden, in Plan B much of it is shaded by trees or man-made structures. This also cuts down on the glare from paved surfaces. In Plan B, decomposed granite was the choice of paving material for the paths because it has a soft, natural color and feel. Patios are covered with hard materials such as paving stones to make a firm support for furniture.

Plants—any kind of plants other than grasses—cover the rest of the ground, and because the area taken up by lawn is now much smaller, there is room for more interesting plantings, from flowers to vegetables. In Plan B any of these is preferred, because almost any plant uses less water than lawn grasses. Once the balance has been shifted away from the lawn, the garden as a whole is a lot more fun— to walk through, to sit or to work in. There is still enough lawn for rough-and-tumble play, or even a game of catch, but it no longer dominates the landscape.

GROUND COVERS AND OTHER OPTIONS

Instead of a lawn in her Santa Monica garden, landscape designer Nancy Goslee Power planted the delightful checkerboard hedge on pages 24-25. It is a bold solution to providing open space in a little town or city garden. A lawn this small would not make much sense, nor would it be very interesting. Two kinds of the drought-tolerant Mediterranean herb santolina make the alternating pattern: the gray is *Santolina chamaecyparissus* and the green is *S. virens.*

Ground Covers Not a Cure-All Ground covers of various kinds are frequently sold as lawn substitutes and they make handsome little meadows if used sparingly. But having too much of the same ground cover is the surest way to make a garden monotonous—and don't think for a minute it has the advantage of being carefree. A ground cover's undoing is the lowly weed, which finds most low-growing plants easy to invade. Once a weed has taken hold, it is almost impossible to get it out of a ground-cover planting. When ground

covers are used in small patches, it is easier to keep an eye on weeds and get into the beds to remove them.

A Case for Ground Covers Ground covers use much less water than a lawn, and a few can do completely without it. In areas where water is precious, tall, spreading, shrubby ground covers are a good choice, especially where there is a great deal of ground to be covered. Landscape architect Robert Fletcher suggests "large, simple drifts of the same plant" for extensive areas, and he is not talking about the traditional ground covers but of shrubby plants that shade the ground and make invasion by weeds' difficult. In test plantings at the University of Arizona, this scheme has been found to be one of the best ways to save water without adding to the heat load of a garden—far more economical with water than a lawn, and much better than paving or gravel mulches for absorbing the sun's heat. These low-growing (two-to-four-feet tall) ground-covering shrubs are planted very far apart, with a thick organic mulch temporarily spread over the ground until the plants fill in. They are planted far apart so they will not grow together too quickly and then mound up higher than they are supposed to be, thus becoming a monstrous maintenance headache. This kind of planting can create a very elegant look while using very little water since each plant can be efficiently irrigated by little drip emitters.

In the Shade One of the best places to plant certain kinds of ground covers is in the shade, where lawns would be difficult to grow. Lawns should always be in sunny spaces, as should most ground covers, but there are a few that will grow happily in shade.

*Sometimes it's appropriate to use every kind of ground cover in combination. The lawn is a somewhat drought-resistant tall fescue. Blue star creeper (*Laurentia fluviatilis*), thyme, and other creepers fill in between the stone pavers.*

Garden Visit

NO LAWN AT ALL

Sometimes a garden is so small that it is best to plan it with no lawn at all, as is the case with this garden in Southern California's San Fernando Valley. The owners wanted flowers and other interesting plants, and since there was just so much space, they opted to omit the conventional lawn.

Garden designer Chris Rosmini couldn't have been more delighted with this request because her gardens are well known for the exuberance of their plant materials, and she "hasn't left anyone with a lawn in years." Her plan for the garden is almost medieval, with the paths that connect all the parts looking remarkably like the oddly angled streets in a medieval town. The main path sets off from the house at an angle, and you must jog over a few feet to get onto it, but the garden is otherwise formal in plan with a definite end and focal point—a gazebo covered with curving copper pipes. Other lesser focal points anchor the ends of less important paths—

small fountains, quiet pools of water in large containers, or plants spilling fountainlike from large pots.

The areas between the paths are planted with all sorts of wonderful growing things, and the beds are raised to make them easier to enjoy, easier to weed, and—because many of these plants are finicky—to provide the best of soil and drainage. Many ornamental grasses provide graceful accents along the paths and in the beds. Note how plants grow at the foot of the raised beds to soften the paths' edges.

To one side of this grid of pathways is a covered patio, just off a greenhouse room, and there are several other turnouts along the paths where you can stop to enjoy views of the garden (all of the raised beds are enclosed by walls, tall and wide enough to sit on). At the center of the garden the paths converge and provide a central piazza. Another garden ornament yet to be decided on (these things take time) will grace this central bed. For the moment, it is full of flowers, with nary a lawn in sight.

Some gardeners wonder why they should waste space with lawns when there are so many prettier plants. Such was the case in this San Fernando Valley garden, where paths provide the open space and carry you between raised beds that are simply stuffed with fascinating plants, including some grasses—though not the kind you mow. The reddish grass so prominent in the beds is a fountain grass, Pennisetum setaceum 'Rubrum.'

CHAPTER

3

BUILDING THE BACKGROUND

On pages 44–45, the autumn gold of a majestic old ginkgo, with the brilliant red patch of annual bedding salvia behind it, looks most dramatic against the rather plain background of green.

A sketch of the garden will quickly show where background is needed. Note how a neighbor's shrub was "borrowed" to deepen the view in the top sketch.

Rather than wall your garden in with shrubs and trees, as in the sketch at the left, try irregular planting schemes, like the one at the right, with bulges and gaps for a more varied and open look.

A FRAME FOR THE GARDEN

Paths tell us where to look in a garden, but once the eye has followed a path to its conclusion it is free to roam, so the next step in planning a garden is to gently guide the eye to what we might most like to look at next. The background helps decide this by obscuring what could be objectionable—a telephone pole or a neighbor's toolshed for instance—and by emphasizing what is attractive. The background itself, be it fence or foliage, is not what you should be looking at. It is there simply to make other things look good, to focus attention on the flowers or on a fish pond—to make them stand out.

The best backgrounds are rather plain. They might be fences, walls, shrubs, or even trees, if something tall needs to be concealed, and they are often a combination of these. Fences and walls take up the least space but make a rather abrupt boundary for the garden. Planting shrubs in front of them, at least in some places, helps soften this boundary. Shrubs by themselves are perhaps the best background for a garden because they don't look so much like an end as an edge. They do not emphatically state "this is the end of the garden," but actually hint that there might be more beyond. This illusion loses its power if they are planted in a rigid row at the very edge of the garden; then they are too much like a wall themselves.

Take Inventory and Borrow Views
Before building this background, take inventory of the view. Decide what you want to see beyond the garden and what you do not. Try not to find everything objectionable on the other side of your property line or you will box yourself in with shrubbery or walls. Does your neighbor have an especially handsome tree or shrub? Do not plant in front of it, but take advantage of the gift. This is what designers call a "borrowed landscape," though they usually borrow more than just one plant. You may find more to borrow, too. There may be a nice view across your neighbor's garden that you can borrow by planting so that it becomes part of your view and appears to become part of your garden. Even in the most cramped garden there are probably distant trees or mountains that you can borrow, and you should emphasize these by framing them with your background. If a mountaintop juts up in the distance, let your background dip to take it in.

What you do not want to see will determine where the background must be the deepest or tallest. Telephone poles are a modern curse and are particularly difficult to hide; while only a tree will do the job, it can't be planted too close to the telephone lines or the utility company will be pruning it for you, and they are not going to care what it looks like when they leave. One way to hide a utility pole is to plant far enough in front of it so that, thanks to perspective, even a smallish tree will hide it. In fact, the background for the garden does not have to be as far back as is physically possible. Lining up shrubs along the property line may enclose the garden so abruptly that it feels smaller than it is. Let the background weave in and out along the property line so it makes a soft edge for the garden, and you will be less aware that there is an edge.

It Takes Room Admittedly, this takes room—most shrubs need at least six to eight feet of width to grow in—but the background is so important to the garden's look and feel that space should be found, even if you must sacrifice some of the lawn. To get some idea of what needs hiding and what doesn't, sketch the view of the garden, perhaps from the back door, or photograph it, have prints made, then draw right on the prints with a grease pencil. Hide what you do not like with sketchy trees or shrubs, thereby emphasizing what you do like—what remains.

Remember, try not to box yourself in by hiding everything. Even if only a blank wall stares back at you from the other side of the property line, it is a few feet further away than anything in your garden and therefore will make your garden seem deeper or wider than it really is. Even a few feet of borrowed scenery let the eye escape from the garden's confines. If the garden space becomes roomlike of necessity, it's nice to have a few windows to look out of.

When you have sketched what the view from the back of the house will look like, walk out into the garden, look back at the house, and see if that view can be improved. Gardens do not have just one view, though one may be the most important because it is the one most seen (the view from the kitchen window, for instance).

The garden can frame the house as well as the view, thereby making the house more a part of the garden. If the walls of the house are too bright or too plain, they can be hidden with tall shrubs or covered with vines. A vine running along the eaves can soften the outline of the house. A small tree can break up the straight line of the roof.

Whatever you do, do not completely ring the house with shrubs. This is called "foundation planting" and is deadly to any design. Let the grass, ground covers, or paving come right up to the walls of the house in some spots and the garden will seem larger because you can see further.

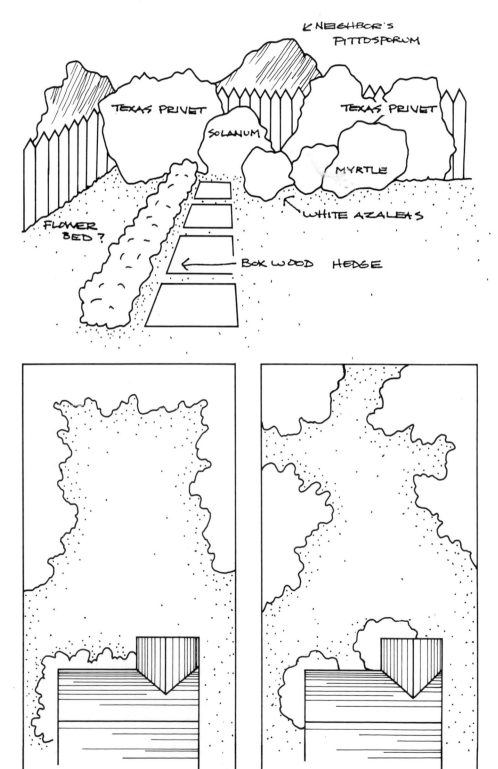

Garden Visit

ALL THE INGREDIENTS

This average-sized backyard has all the ingredients of a good garden. There is a strong path down one side, wide, ample, and as straight as an arrow. A meadowlike lawn flows roughly in the same direction as the garden walk and augments the path as another way to get to the various corners of the garden (though the most heavily worked section can be reached by the path). The lawn, edged by the path and a patio, grows in full sun, so it is healthy and happy. It is just large enough to open up the garden, but not so large that it overwhelms it. There are strong focal points, in this case the mushroom-like straddlestones brought from the Cotswolds in England (where they were used inside piles of hay so air could circulate and keep the stacks

The view from the living room on this page, framed by an umbrella of ivy, encourages the eye to dart to a focal point, the mushroom-shaped straddlestone, purchased in England and now comfortably at home in Pasadena. Tall, bearded iris make a dramatic foil for the stone.

Every nook and cranny is planted, and where there is no soil there are containers brimming with primroses and a white streptocarpus.

The view from the garden back to the house is framed by roses and a red bottlebrush tree. In the distance, a climbing Lady Banks rose helps the arbor harmonize with the rest of the garden. The handsome reddish foliage still further in the background is the neighbor's purple-leaf plum, borrowed to good effect by the gardener. The straddlestones are cleverly used to carry the eye across the garden as lily pads do a frog across a pond.

from rotting). Surrounded by creeping ranunculus, the interesting stones give the eye something to look at right away, while the general profusion of the garden sinks in.

The substantial background of leafy green plants makes the flowers stand out and screens out the neighbors without making the garden feel cramped. A purple-leaf plum in one corner keeps this background from becoming monotonous, and it is worth noting how it adds to the apparent depth of the background planting; it seems much further away than the other property-line shrubs. Though this is a garden for someone who loves flowers and interesting foliage (and uses them in grand bouquets in the house), there is a place to sit in the garden, even room to entertain.

The paving materials have a texture and color that go with the earthy look of the place—decomposed granite (or "d.g." for short) covering the path, and rough bricks making the patio. A clever planting of ivy trained over an old umbrella frame helps the patio look a little special and neatly crops the view of the garden from the house. Seen from the patio, the ivy planting helps to hide part of the two-story house.

The flowers grow in beds that are large enough for them to develop luxuriantly and with a wide variety of heights and textures, greatly adding to the beds' interest. And when one has exhausted the obvious visual treats, there is yet another level of detail— pretty plants tucked here and there, or in pots, waiting to be discovered on second look. This is a gardener's garden (it belongs to Joan Banning), in a gardener's town (Pasadena), where even the humble garden hose has an honored place and looks completely at home.

For colors to come alive, they need to be viewed against a simple background. Here, citrus and other plain green shrubs make the colors in this border pop out. The flowers include tall delphiniums, bright yellow coreopsis, and red penstemon. This border is typical of many in California in the way in which it mixes annuals with perennials to good effect.

KEEP IT SIMPLE AND LEAVE ENOUGH ROOM

The background for a garden should not distract from the garden's features, nor should it be too obvious. If it is too strong, it will tend to constrict the space; if too complicated, it will compete with the things that you really want to look at, be they flowers or a splashing fountain. The importance of a background is obvious in photographs. The next time you look at a garden picture in a magazine or book, take note of the background and see how plain it is. Photographers speak of "separation." The plants they are photographing must "separate" from their background—they must stand out— or the whole composition becomes a hodgepodge. What works for the camera usually works for the eye.

Shrubs Are Best Shrubs are the best possible background because their green color makes them a part of the garden and harmonizes with other plantings. The best background shrubs should be dark green with leaves of medium size, neither too big and bold, nor too small and delicate. If they flower, those flowers should be small and inconspicuous; most shrubs used for background plantings have simple little white flowers.

Although it is tempting to use shrubs that are colorful, remember that as a background they tend to draw too much attention to themselves. It is far more dramatic to let the plants in front steal the show. Flowers seen against a simple, dark green background seem to have colors that glow, and the various textures of other plants are more dramatic against the simple texture of the background plantings. If you want to use flowering shrubs, put them in front of plainer shrubs, but this brings

up another rule of background plantings—give them enough room.

Shrubs Grow Big If a shrub is going to grow tall enough to be a backdrop, it is also going to spread laterally. Though a few shrubs do grow taller than they are wide, most need room to grow naturally into a rounded shape. Too often we don't give them this room and end up having to take them out a few years later, or we have to take out the pruning shears. As soon as we start pruning, we no longer have naturally graceful shrubs for a background, but clipped hedges, not a harmonious setting for flowers that show best in a more casual environment.

Of course you want to have as much open space in the garden as possible, but it isn't necessary to have a great deal and the sacrifices made to get it outweigh any benefits. Do we really need all that empty space, which is usually planted to lawn? Yet in most gardens, plants are pushed as close to the property lines as is physically possible, as if we were clearing the floor of furniture for a dance.

Give Plants Their Place Instead, vow to give plants their place and enough space to grow without constraint. Start thinking of an eight-foot-wide swath as just about the minimum for the background shrubs, and later be prepared to give flowers and other plants equally generous quarters. If you simply haven't the room for this graceful background of unclipped shrubs, then plant shrubs that can be pruned as hedges; but even these need at least three to four feet of garden space. If all else fails to fit, resort to walls and fences, which should also be simple and plain when used as a backdrop for the garden. Elaborate designs have their place, but not in the background.

"I Didn't Know It Would Grow that Big" In my garden you often hear, "it wasn't supposed to grow that big," a lament all too common, I suspect. In my grandfather's day (he was a landscape architect), plants were spaced far apart, and it took years for them to grow together. There was a lot of empty space between the circles that represented plants on his plans. That is one reason old gardens—especially estate gardens—often look more majestic than modern ones. Plants weren't crowded and could grow to their natural size, without unnatural pruning. Trees could become monumental in size because enough room was allowed. Shrubs could grow and spread, making an elegant and dense green backdrop for the rest of the garden. There was plenty of time.

In this impatient age, we plant everything too closely together because we want a garden to look finished within a reasonable amount of time (next week is not too soon). Trees get crowded and have to be taken out long before their time. Shrubs planted close to one another grow together so they become more like a hedge and need constant pruning. Most of us don't even know what some of the most common shrubs really look like, because they are never given the room to assume their natural shape. I don't think we modern gardeners are completely to blame. Circumstances do force us to keep moving on, and few of us can expect to spend more than five or ten years in one place, yet that is the time it takes for a plant to reach a reasonable size.

Landscape designers have a way around this: plant twice what you will eventually need, and when the flowers or shrubs have grown and begin to touch, take out every other one. Don't wait too long or they will begin to

shade each other and lose their lower leaves and branches. When you take out the temporary plants, you will again have holes in your scheme, but now the remaining plants can continue to grow and fill in. There is also this rare thing called patience. Sometimes, for the sake of privacy, a fence or wall can be a better choice, with some of the best slow-growing shrubs or trees in front of it. You just need to wait a little. Something can also be said for a little air between plants. They tend to look better, get more sun on their lower branches, and are healthier because good air circulation is important to plants.

Knowing just how large something will become can be a problem. When a garden book says, "grows to six or ten feet," figure on ten. Since I am always trying to fit a few more plants in the garden, I accept the lower number, but the plant often reaches that size in a year or two. The description of the ordinary *Pittosporum tobira* in the *Sunset Western Garden Book* shows how vague the published size of a plant can be: "Broad, dense shrub or small tree, 6–15 feet tall, rarely 30 ft." Before I learned better, I would have counted on six feet, but what would have happened to my garden if it had grown to thirty?

So it seems that plants that grow too big are a part of modern gardening, but there is help on its way. Nurseries are busy developing and introducing smaller, more compact, plants, from annuals to trees, but especially shrubs. A good example is a new dwarf variegated *Pittosporum tobira*, named Turner's Variegated Dwarf. Most people give the regular variegated pittosporum about six feet to grow in because at least one garden book says it grows to "about 5 ft. high and as broad," but mine grew that tall and

wide in two years. In one garden, I saw it about eight feet tall and a good fifteen feet across. It took up most of the backyard. This shrub is always planted in too little space, but let's hope Turner's Variegated Dwarf lives up to its billing and is a lot smaller!

Plants that grow bigger than the space I have allowed them have caused me a lot of hard work. Each time I take something out, I have to start all over again in that spot, but I'm learning. I now look up the size of each plant and then write the size on the plant label, where it stares me right in the face so I can't ignore it at planting time. I also get out a tape measure and see if the plant will really fit. I still cheat some, but I am getting better and a little more patient. And patience is one of gardening's gentle lessons.

PERSPECTIVE, PROPORTION, BALANCE, AND THE RULE OF THREE'S AND FIVE'S

Some basic rules of design make the planning of any garden planting a whole lot easier. You can use these rules when planting trees or shrubs for the background, for flowers, bulbs, and ground covers. The easiest to explain is what I call "the rule of three's and five's"—three of anything look better than one or two, and five look even better. The temptation is to plant just one of everything because at the nursery one tends to buy just one of this and one of that; or, to go the opposite route and plant a field full from nursery flats, because it's easier than trying to plan a planting scheme in advance.

The first extreme makes for a lot of odd fellows, and the other gets boring pretty quickly. Instead, try buying three or five of everything, or similar odd-numbered combinations. You can

There is nothing like practice to hone a technique. To practice some of the rules of composition, purchase a variety of foam balls at a florist's supply store and arrange them this way and that. Here, a pair of balls is contrasted with three of a kind, the pair looking stiff and formal, the three more natural.

Small in front of large (lower photos) is not nearly as dramatic an arrangement as large in front of small; note how far away the small ball looks when placed behind a large one.

practice this rule with any object: I've even used foam balls to illustrate this point; or on a piece of paper, draw circles to represent plants. But in a sketch you lose the third dimension that makes gardens such a rich experience.

Try Some Combinations Make up combinations of three's and five's and see how pleasing they appear. What hap-

pens is that odd-numbered combinations tend to balance each other in an eccentric fashion—they simply look more natural. Before you actually plant anything in the ground, put the candidates, in their nursery containers, where they are to be planted and look at them for a while. Arrange them into groups and then rearrange them, imagining how they will look in terms of their size in a few years. Keep moving them around until they look pleasing. It's a lot easier to rearrange them at this point than it is after they are in the ground, so take your time and wait a few days to see if you still feel the same about their relationship.

For a Formal Look If you are not after a natural look, then balance your plantings precisely. For a distinctly formal walk put one plant on one side, and an identical plant on the other—instant formality. But I suspect you'll be happier with plantings that look informal and natural, even if the path is not. One trick is to make most of the plantings informal, but where you want to emphasize something—a gate perhaps —suddenly use a formally arranged pair of plants.

Balance Balance is a little trickier to explain, but if you think of any plant of a given size as having weight, you will begin to see how plants might balance one another. If you plant three shrubs that are each going to grow to three feet across, they will be in balance with two shrubs that each grow to about five feet across. Both groups of plants have about the same visual weight and are in balance. If you think I just broke the rule of three's and five's by suggesting that you plant two shrubs, I sort of did, but by balancing the two against the three, I came up with a total of five, so you can see that balance modifies this rule and makes it more versatile. Try it with the foam balls and see if it doesn't look right.

Perhaps the reason such planting looks right is that in nature plants tend to grow in colonies: one plant gets its start and then spreads underground or drops seed around itself—soon it's a colony of plants. However, seldom do they so get the upper hand on other plants that they completely dominate

an area. They learn to share, and what you see in nature is one colony growing next to another, then another next to that, and so on, in a well-balanced fashion. The rule of three's and five's seeks to imitate this look.

Scale and Proportion Scale and proportion enter into garden planning, specifically when the natural parts of a garden are close to the man-made.

A narrow little planting bed right next to the massive bulk of a house is out of proportion and is going to give the garden a puny look, making the house bulky and domineering. A wider bed with larger plants in it, makes the transition between house and garden smoother—things are in proportion.

Perspective Perspective can be tinkered with and should be considered.

A small object in front of a large object looks as if it is close; put it behind the large object and it looks further away than it actually is and since it appears further away, the garden seems larger. This is called "forcing the perspective," and it's a particularly useful trick along a path or sight line, yet most of us tend to do the opposite. We put the smallest plants in the foreground and the largest way in back, thinking that we get privacy at the property line. So keep an eye open for someplace where you can force that perspective—the illusion of space is as good as having those few extra feet.

You can also force the perspective by using just the foliage of plants. Put large-leaved plants in the foreground and small-leaved plants in the background. Those little leaves will look a lot further away from the large leaves than they actually are.

ACCENT AND SURPRISE

Sometimes you should break the rule of three's and five's outright and plant just one plant—it's going to stick out like a sore thumb so it had better be special. But this is a great way to emphasize a favorite plant. It would not be possible without the rule of three's and five's, which makes a foil for that favorite plant—that one must be the exception, not the rule. Designers call these special plantings "accents," and they are important to the garden's design because they are supplementary focal points. In any given part of the garden, accents are the first thing you look at and they help to establish an order: First you look down your path and see the focal point at its end; as the eye begins to wander over the rest of the garden, these accent plants catch your attention and hold it momentarily.

Spires and Steeples Sometimes accent plants are not single specimens. They may be a group of plants that are quite different in shape but tend to be viewed as one object. The most obvious distinctive shape is one that is tall and lean, that towers above the generally rounded shape of other plants—spires and steeples in the village of more ordinary plants. Italian cypress are often used this way on a large scale, hollyhocks and delphiniums on a smaller scale. Their sheer verticality draws the necessary attention, delphiniums so dramatically it is difficult for me to imagine a garden without them.

Accent plants have an element of surprise to them, which makes them and the garden they grace more delightful. They may be surprisingly beautiful, or tall, or graceful, or an astonishing color.

Surprise Surprise can be an important part of any garden, but it is often lacking. A large expanse of unrelieved lawn holds no surprise. It may be elegant and lush, yet everyone knows that there is nothing unexpected out there. But let it curve around a clump of shrubs, and the possibility exists that something surprising is around the corner, just out of sight—perhaps a planting of those delphiniums waiting to be discovered, a garden pool, a pleasant bench under a tree, or an inviting swing hanging from that tree. Whatever it is, it shouldn't be immediately visible or it won't come as a surprise.

Even in formal garden plans, there is a way to create surprise. The path, just wide enough to allow passage, could disappear through a hedge just tall enough to block the view of what is beyond, and the surprise would be waiting on the other side.

More garden composition practice: Three and five are magic numbers in the design of plantings. In the upper left two large plants harmonize with three smaller ones, for a total of five.

Add a sixth plant that is decidedly different in color or size and it becomes the star, what is called an "accent."

Rather than line shrubs up stiffly, like soldiers guarding the walls of the house (or along a fence), use a variety of sizes.

At the lower right, small shrubs are placed beneath the windows, while a larger one is planted in front of the blank portion of the wall.

Two tall foam tubes add an element of surprise and excitement to the foam ball composition. A jet of water, a tall thin plant or tree, a sculpture, can add similar excitement to the plantings in the garden.

In Hortense Miller's garden in Laguna Beach, tall, old-fashioned hollyhocks prove they are still among the most surprising and delightful plants. Their companions are pink Mexican evening primrose and golden coreopsis.

Too Much of a Good Thing Classical gardens made good use of surprise, often employing hedges and little passages, though sometimes the surprise was a little too much. The Italians loved to put hidden jets of water here and there that came on all of a sudden and soaked visitors. Even the normally restrained English overdid surprise in their gracious, quiet gardens, building ludicrous structures called "follies" that one stumbles upon on a tour of the garden—lacquer-red Chinese towers or carefully built castle ruins. Today, some of these follies still catch a visitor by surprise—perhaps "shock" better describes one's astonishment.

"Surprise" can quickly become "sore thumb" so restraint is called for. At the least, limit the surprises to one per garden area.

Plant Portrait

THOSE TOWERING DELPHINIUMS

My grandfather, a pioneer landscape architect in the San Francisco area, might not have been impressed, but he certainly would have been pleased to see my delphiniums. His delphiniums, like his rhododendrons, tuberous begonias, and fuchsias, were the kind beside which you could proudly pose. In his fading Kodachromes, the rhododendron trusses are as large as Louis Smaus's hatted head, the tuberous begonias not much smaller. And the delphiniums? They tower above everything like New England church steeples, brilliantly colored, as though painted by Portuguese fishermen.

My grandfather was a close friend of Frank Reinelt, the creator of modern delphiniums. Both were schooled in horticulture in the European tradition, in Czechoslovakia, and both apprenticed in the gardens of queens—in Reinelt's case Queen Marie of Rumania. Lured by the feats of the legendary Luther Burbank, Reinelt and my grandfather came to California in the early 1900s. My grandfather designed landscapes for the Spreckels and other San Francisco families; Reinelt designed flowers by hybridizing and selecting, creating the first dinner-plate-size tuberous begonias, the Pacific strain of primroses, and the Pacific strain of delphiniums—all of which are still the standard of perfection.

These delphiniums were the first to rival the developments of the great European hybridizers, primarily because they encompassed so many blues—brilliant blue, sky blue, robin's egg blue, blue as dark and clear as sapphires. Many had a contrasting "bee" at their center, either as black as a carpenter bee (which was neatly concealed, to my occasional surprise)

or pure white. There was nothing purplish about these flowers. They were *blue*.

The Pacific series, sometimes called Pacific Giants, is a "strain," and although the concept of a seed strain is a little confusing, it distinguishes how we in California grow delphiniums from the way they are grown in Europe. There, delphiniums are almost permanent plants. Named kinds are propagated from divisions and persist in the garden for years, becoming ever larger clumps until they must be divided and then replanted. In California, Reinelt discovered, delphiniums don't persist, even though they are perennial plants. So he developed strains that could be grown almost like annuals—sow the seed, move the young plants into the garden, and they bloom. When they're finished, pull them out and start over again. A strain is born after much crossing, when the progenies of each generation become enough alike to be called similar. Plants grown from a seed strain are not identical, but they are supposed to be nearly so. In Reinelt's case, the Pacific strains were near perfect—identical in height, color, and form. Developed between 1938 and 1940, these strains received Best of Show gold medal at the 1939 Oakland Spring Flower Show, the premier West Coast show of its time—a measure of their importance and popularity. Most of his strains are still with us, although they have deteriorated somewhat through the years. It is the nature of strains that they must be carefully and laboriously recrossed periodically to keep them strong and uniform, and that has been difficult.

The true blue strains are the Bluejay series and Summer Skies series. Other less blue or outright purple strains have names chosen from Alfred Tennyson's "Idylls of the King,"

Delphiniums, such as this towering member of the Pacific Giant strain, bring instant drama to a garden.

including the King Arthur series, Guinevere, Galahad, Lancelot, Black Knight, and the Round Table series (all of the colors from some 300 crosses).

The Pacific strains grow to a height of at least six feet, and it is not difficult to find photographs of Pacific Giants growing eight feet tall. They are usually used in a big way. I have a fading blueprint of my grandfather's design for a Hillsborough estate in Northern California which contains a delightful double border on either side of an ample path leading to a formal rose garden. These borders contain a brilliant mix of flowers and fruit trees that I plan to copy someday. But the borders are big—the reason for my delay in duplicating them. They are each 100 feet in length and eight feet wide, and there is a separate foot-wide border of ageratum, aubrieta, iberis, and petunia 'Rosey Morn' in front of the main border. The borders are so big that there is a tiny paved path behind each for access. The delphiniums are toward the back, and each of the five plantings occupies an area of about four by seven feet.

In this grand scheme, the importance of a big, strapping strain of delphiniums is evident. The delphiniums are planted in pockets between flowering fruit trees, which are "underplanted" with daffodils for spring bloom, and then with chrysanthemums, "grown on and transplanted" for fall bloom. The beds of tall delphiniums balance the weight of the fruit trees. Behind the delphiniums are plantings of watsonia, which bloom while the delphiniums are still small— just a bushy foreground. As the bulbs fade, the growing delphiniums hide the drying watsonia foliage.

To either side of the delphiniums in one planting are nicotiana and a phlox named 'Elizabeth Campbell'; nearby

are plantings of scabiosa—another fine blue flower—and iris, presumably blue. In another planting, the companions are *Salvia pitcheri*, trachelium, and *Penstemon barbatus*. In another, it is the carmine-flowered *Lilium speciosum* 'Rubrum' and phlox 'Miss Lingard' beside a flowering peach; and in still another, anthemis, doronicum, and daylilies.

The colors of the delphiniums were not specified, nor how many were to be planted, but a dozen plants in each pocket was probably close, and each planting probably contained but one color, since mad mixes were not the fashion. A clever gardener could probably guess the color of the delphiniums by the colors of the plants nearby, but, in general, it seems that most were blue contrasting with pink and red, or purple next to soft yellows.

That is how my grandfather used delphiniums professionally, but in his own modest bungalow garden in Burlingame he grew them in narrow beds just outside a sunny breakfast nook, where I remember having toast with apricot jam. There the delphiniums and other plants were not so much a composition as they were a display, like the exhibitions at the flower shows he judged. He didn't care that they were out of scale with the house, but was more concerned with size and perfection. He grew everything big and without blemish.

In my garden the delphiniums don't exactly tower. For many years my modern sensibilities kept me from growing delphiniums at all, because they simply seemed too big for the space at hand—until the advent of the Blue Fountains. This strain of short delphiniums was depicted as uniform, about three to four feet tall, and, of course, the blue-flowered sorts were prominently pictured in seed cata-

In a Santa Monica garden a colorful mixture of fall-planted annuals and perennials blooms in April. Annuals include nemesia, petunias, Shirley poppies, snapdragons, Sweet William, and anemones. Shasta daisies, Canterbury bells, columbines, and delphiniums are some of the perennials, though it is the delphiniums that steal the show. The spotted foliage belongs to Abutilon pictum *'Thompsonii.' Believe it or not, this flower bed is only seven months old.*

logues. I suppose that I should have known better than to believe the catalogue pictures, for so far they have been anything but uniform. Every plant is a complete surprise. Some grow two feet tall, some six feet. Some have stems as thick as a giant sequoia; some are as delicate as the wild *Delphinium cardinale* that grows in our chaparral. Some have fat spikes of closely set flowers; others are airy, much like the annual larkspurs.

They are not at all formal flowers, but give more the effect of a country-cottage garden; nor would they have won anything but a polite nod from the judges of the 1939 Oakland Show. I don't believe it's my fault; it's just not a very good strain by Reinelt's standards. Still, I'm delighted with my delphiniums. Passersby compliment me on my garden, even though I know that they are staring only at the delphiniums. And my English neighbors call it an English garden, simply, I suspect, because the delphiniums are there.

Blue Fountains, although far from perfect, is a useful strain because the plants fit into a modern, small flower bed. I can squeeze a dozen Blue Fountains between the roses and my modest collection of perennials. Although very few have turned out to be a true blue, they are blue enough, and the many purples are quite handsome with the purple *Salvia farinacea* and the lilac-colored veronica. The few blues make for a dramatic background for the pink dianthus and the pink and red roses.

I've grown the Blue Fountains strain of delphiniums for several years and have developed a method. I plant them only a foot apart in clusters of several. The soil is laboriously prepared in advance, dug to a foot or more, with peat moss and Gromulch mixed in so that a handful of soil, after being

squeezed in a fist, crumbles apart on its own. A small fistful of Osmocote fertilizer is thrown into the bottom of each hole. That fertilizer, which looks like fish eggs, releases nutrients slowly so that the plants are fed for most of spring and summer.

Planted in that fashion, plants simply shoot up—the results are stupendous. If you had the time, you could probably sit and watch them grow. They seem to bloom within days of planting, although my garden notebook says they were planted in late January and that the first buds opened on April 5. After the main spikes flower, secondary spikes last into summer. The main spikes catch the blooming of the roses, veronicas, dianthus, and other spring flowers, and the secondary spikes bloom along with the early summer flowers, including agapanthus and Shasta daisies.

I plant my delphiniums from four-inch pots (gallon-can-sized plants bloom poorly). I do not grow them from seed, although that is the best way to start delphiniums. In the cultural directions in the Vetterle & Reinelt catalogue of 1940, it is suggested that seed sown from June into September will produce early spring flowers; seed sown in December and January, midsummer flowers; and seed sown from February to April, fall flowers. That would make an interesting experiment if you wanted delphiniums nearly year round.

The cultural description in the catalogue continues with how to get a second set of blooms, and there is no mystery here much to my disappointment. I thought I had discovered a trick, a bit of garden sorcery, in an old book on delphiniums from that golden era of California gardening before World War II. It suggested cutting back the flower spikes so that only a

single leaf remained at the base. Aha!—just a single leaf—so that's the trick. I tried it and within two months the delphiniums were again in full bloom—in late summer.

A year or two later and in a lazier mood, I simply cut the spikes off above the leaves so that quite a few leaves remained and, of course, the plants rebloomed just as well—maybe even better. Reinelt's catalogue suggests to simply cut off the spikes, leaving all the leaves at the base, and then keep the plants on the dry side for two to three weeks, so they are forced to rest. When new shoots appear above ground, cut off the remainder of the old spike. Then sprinkle a teaspoon of ammonium phosphate around the base of each plant, rake it into the soil, and water thoroughly. Further, remove all but two or three of the strongest new shoots from each clump so that they will grow stronger, but I have found that an impossible task, and I rather like the airy quality of the many-spiked second bloom.

Outside of California, where these delphiniums have a better than even chance of returning in following years, the spikes should be cut after flowering and all but four or five of the new sprouts should be removed at the base. Grown as perennials, they should be spaced further apart—24 to 30 inches.

The Pacific types are usually planted from four-inch pots in the fall so they have all winter to gather the strength required for their spectacular growth. In other respects their culture is the same as for the smaller Blue Fountains that are in my garden, except that they almost always need a supporting wooden stake.

Although my grandfather and Frank Reinelt are gone, the Pacific strain survives. One of these days, I will find the room to grow them.

A SHRUB PALETTE

At this point in the planning process it's time to develop a palette of background plants. It is surprising how few gardeners know their shrubs, but it is easy enough to learn, and the learning process is pretty much the same for other plants you will need later on. A walk around the block and a trip to the nursery are good ways to start.

A Walk Around the Block On the walk around the block, you'll see what others have used for shrubs. Take note of their situation—are they growing in sun or shade, or in something in between? Are they on the south, north, or maybe west side of the house? Especially note their size, their width in particular, and, of course, whether they indeed make good backgrounds. It doesn't matter that you don't know what these shrubs are called, because you can next head to a nursery and simply look for the same plant. Find the plant tag, and now that you know its name jot it down in your garden notebook along with your observations, and you have the beginnings of a shrub palette.

If your neighborhood offers slim pickings, try another, or go to a botanic garden and see what they use, but the closer to home you find the examples, the more likely they will work well in your garden. You're not looking for outstanding specimens at this time, so it doesn't matter that you and your neighbors are all growing the same plants. There aren't that many background shrubs to choose from—plain and deep green in color with medium-sized leaves and inconspicuous flowers.

Notoriously Optimistic If you ask someone for recommendations, or begin looking through a book, be aware that any plant that is said to grow fast and thereby sounds ideal for the job is probably ill-suited. Speedy plants are seldom good in any other way. They tend to become trees in a short time, have aggressive root systems that can make growing anything else near them impossible, and often are not dense enough to make a good backdrop or provide the privacy you seek. The shrubs may make spectacular growth, but they don't do anything else well. Also, be aware that books notoriously, or perhaps optimistically, underestimate the eventual size of plants.

Four for Your Notebook They are simply shrubs. There is nothing colorful, unusual, or spectacular about their foliage, while their flowers are plain basic white. But what the four shrubs pictured on pages 66 and 67 do well is form that dark green background you need for other plants. If the flowers in your garden lack a certain punch, it is probably because they don't have the correct background. Roses, perennials, and annual flowers will appear more dramatic against this background of deep green foliage. Light green, gray green, or reddish or bronze-green won't do. These shrubs draw attention to themselves and no longer serve as a backdrop. What we're talking about is an unobtrusive—but substantial—green shrub.

Not surprisingly, several of these simple green shrubs have long been appreciated. They have been favored since Roman times for the cooling effect that their dark green foliage brings to the sunbaked gardens of the Mediterranean, though all four shrubs can tolerate a fair amount of shade. But where they excel is in sunny locations.

These shrubs can also be pruned to shape and they make fine hedges. All are easy to grow and readily available. However, nursery plants are often root-bound from sitting unnoticed in a corner too long, and it is sometimes best to order fresh plants.

PRIVETS The privet of Italian Renaissance and Roman gardens was *Ligustrum vulgare*. More often planted in California is the Japanese privet, *L. japonicum*, especially the cultivar 'Texanum', which is a low grower (six to eight feet). 'Rotundifolium' is another even lower (to five feet) cultivar, and 'Suwannee River' is supposedly lower still (to four feet).

MYRTLES Another Mediterranean plant with a long history. *Myrtus communis* has glossy, green leaves with a most pleasant scent. It grows to about six feet and is most often seen as a hedge, though it makes a handsome, small background shrub. Cultivars such as 'Boetica' and 'Compacta' are smaller, with slightly different foliage.

VIBURNUM Laurustinus, *Viburnum tinus*, also dates from Roman days. It grows to six or ten feet, in time maybe even taller. In winter, the tiny white flowers are deliciously fragrant, though subtle. In appearance, it is a slightly less formal shrub.

PRUNUS An American native, the Carolina laurel cherry, *Prunus caroliniana*, grows fast and is exceptionally neat and regular from day one—particularly the cultivars 'Compacta' and 'Bright 'n Tight'. The eventual height is between ten feet—if it's pruned as a hedge—to twenty feet when left alone. This one does best near the ocean or in partial shade far inland.

Your Own List These four shrubs were most recommended by landscape designers for use in California gardens; some also work well in other parts of the country, and there are certainly other candidates for other climates.

Landscape designers like simple shrubs for background plantings and these are some of their choices for California: sweet-smelling lauristinus (upper left), Japanese privet (upper right), Carolina laurel cherry (lower left), and the old favorite, myrtle (lower right), with its fragrant foliage. Other areas have their own preferences, but background shrubs should always be plain.

Plant Portrait

EARLY CAMELLIAS

You've probably observed in your own garden that some camellias bloom earlier than others—and these are an especially valuable lot simply because they bloom before the big spring rush when so much else does, and they are more noticeable. In California the peak of the season comes during March, but the camellias pictured here bloom in January and early February, the middle of winter. The sasanqua camellias bloom even earlier, but their blooms are generally smaller and decidedly less fancy, and the bushes are a trifle stiff and sticklike. The camellias shown here are all japonica types, with full-blown, full-size flowers on neat, dense bushes. Only the japonicas are capable of such variation—from the unusual tulip-shaped flowers of 'Tulip Time' to the complex geometry of 'Donnan's Dream'. In between are all sorts of camellia forms—semi-doubles, anemone or peony forms, variegated, and picotees.

It is the nature of early camellias to begin flowering a month or more before they reach their peak—slowly opening blooms that tend to last, thus making a more consistent showing in the garden. In comparison, midseason camellias (most are classified as such) open all at once, and though they make more of a splash, it is short-lived. The early varieties are often the prettiest and most perfect because they open when the weather is cool and mild, and therefore most camellia shows are held early in the season. These early camellias are ideal candidates for the backs of flower borders, where they can be in the shade of taller shrubs and trees, and are first-class background shrubs.

For this purpose, their colors couldn't be more suitable. The soft pinks and whites are perfect for the season and complement many spring flowers as they start to bloom. Imagine them behind the tall spikes of larkspur, Canterbury bells, bachelor's buttons, dianthus, or stock. By the time your summer garden is in bloom, camellia bushes are a glossy, deep-green backdrop for that season's warmer colors.

Camellias like shade, though not too much of it. They are one of the few shrubs that can thrive in a garden where they will have winter shade and summer sun. The north side of most California houses would be bare were it not for camellias. There they can be planted as a background for primroses and cinerarias, or they can stand alone with ferns and other shady plants at their feet.

A nice thing about camellias is that they should be planted during their season of bloom, so you can actually see what you are getting. Prepare the soil thoroughly by digging in quantities of organic matter. Camellias do most of their growing immediately after flowering, so be sure to add some fertilizer to the bottom of the planting holes. Also, take care to plant the camellia bush a bit high so that the top of the root ball sits about a half-inch above the soil level. The after-planting regimen calls for fertilizing every other month from right after flowering until early fall, when the buds are formed for next season's blossoms.

Camellia petal blight is a fairly common disease on camellias, though not as common as some suspect. Many other problems are called petal blight, but true petal blight is easily recognized because the petals become watery and soft. The only cure is cultural: rake up all fallen petals after bloom and dispose of them. The idea is to try to prevent the disease from returning or spreading, and it usually takes several years of effort.

Some camellias bloom early in the season when little else is in flower. The early bloomers include the varieties, 'Tulip Time' with its unusual bell-like flowers at the upper left; the incredible 'Donnan's Dream' with its perfect symmetry at the upper right; the frilly 'Kick-off' at the lower left; and 'Amabel Lansdell' at the lower right.

Plant Portrait

NOT YOUR ORDINARY AZALEA

Every flower is a surprise on certain Satsuki azaleas. Some varieties have flowers that are rimmed in a contrasting color or have a collar of white, others have flowers that are solid or variously striped, deep or softly colored, or tipped in a contrasting color— all on the same plant. Satsuki azaleas are not your ordinary azaleas. The sampling pictured here merely hints at the possibilities.

Satsuki azaleas are complex, age-old hybrids of several azaleas native to the mountains of Japan, and they have been trickling into the United States by following what could be called the "bonsai pipeline," since Satsukis are mostly grown by bonsai enthusiasts. But what began as a trickle may soon become a flood as more people discover Satsukis for their gardens. They make good bonsai subjects, because they are naturally compact plants. A five-year-old Satsuki will have grown only about two-and-one-half feet tall and three feet wide, a nearly perfect size for today's gardens. Satsuki means "fifth month," which is when they bloom—in May and early June—a whole month or more after other kinds of azaleas have finished. Already Nuccio's Nurseries, the camellia and azalea specialists in Altadena, California, offers several pages of Satsukis in the catalogue, including several of their own hybrids as well as those

shown here. And there are hundreds
more grown in Japan, where Satsukis
have a devoted following.

The more you learn of Satsukis, the
better they sound. Because of their
compact size, they are unusually dense
and rounded. The foliage is a dark
green, sometimes flushed with bronze.
The leaves of many varieties turn as
brilliant as Japanese maples in fall
(some bloom again at that time),
though since the plants are not deciduous only the older leaves drop off.
The leaves are leathery and tough;
Satsukis can stand quite a bit of sun. At
Nuccio's, where the summer temperatures soar and the sun bakes the surrounding chaparral, many Satsukis are
grown in the open. The best situation

is one with morning or filtered sun.

Like other azaleas, however, they
need a richly prepared, acidic soil and
ample moisture, yet they must have
the best drainage. Add lots of organic
matter (peat moss is preferred, but
commercial azalea planting mixes are
available also). A six-inch layer tilled
into the top foot of soil is not excessive.
Some gardeners go even further, planting in soil that is almost entirely
amendment and in raised beds.

The unusually colored and marked
blooms are the result of "sporting"—
when branches that appear seemingly
out of nowhere grow flowers not seen
elsewhere on the plant. Those are
propagated to produce new varieties.
Some branches may even "sport" on

your own plant—they do so easily.
Once in a while, however, branches,
especially those having flowers with
contrasting borders, revert after planting, so what you see is not necessarily
what you get. There is an element of
chance.

The most spectacular Satsukis are
those casually called "multicolored".
Like the variety shown here named
'Shinsen', they may have some flowers
of a solid color, others of a lighter
shade of the same color, many striped
or speckled with both shades plus
white, and some almost entirely white.
And as we said, each flower is a surprise, because you never know what
will open or where it will show up on
the bush.

One of the new, smaller shrubs is Pit-tosporum tobira 'Wheeler's Dwarf,' on page 72. There is an even newer variegated variety with cream-striped leaves.

The pure red abutilon on page 73 is one of the best shrubs for shady gardens, growing to about six feet around with large bell-like flowers that bloom all winter and spring. It, unfortunately, has no specific name.

Hydrangeas, too, are great in the shade. The one on the far right is a so-called lace-cap. The lacy center never opens any further, which gives the shrub an airy look when in flower.

A FEW MORE PLANTS FOR THE SHADE

Shady parts of the garden pose their own problems and require their own palette of plants. In particular, the north side of the house presents diffi-culties: while it is in shadow all winter, it is likely to be bathed in sun during the hottest time of the year, as the sun climbs higher in the summer months. Camellias and to a lesser extent azaleas excel on the north side of the house and can be the backbone of any shady garden, though neither of them will bloom well in deep shade. The north side of the house is not in what garden-ers term "dense shade" because that side is open to the sky overhead so though there is plenty of light, there is just no direct sun.

Hydrangeas, another candidate for a shady garden, are especially valu-able because they flower after the camellias and azaleas, carrying the show of color into summer. If you want a blue hydrangea, you had better buy it in flower. Hydrangeas must be turned blue in California because that color results from acid soil—ours is at best neutral and at worst alkaline. In New Zealand and in Seattle, where the soils are quite acid, hydrangeas natu-rally turn a bright—even brilliant— blue. If you scatter aluminum sulfate (sold at nurseries) around the base of a hydrangea before it makes buds, and then once again when the buds are about half-size, you might make the flowers turn blue.

In my experience, however, not all hydrangeas will become blue in acid soil, so it is best to buy one that is blue to begin with. Otherwise, you will have pink hydrangeas—unfortunately not a soft baby pink but a rather unpleasant

shade of the color. You can also take the safe route and plant a white-flowered hydrangea.

Camellias, azaleas, and hydrangeas, as do most shade plants, like a rich, porous soil similar to what you find on a forest floor. Before planting, mix into your bed bags of organic soil amendment such as redwood or ground bark. I usually till in a six-inch layer of amendment, that has been spread on top, to a depth of about a foot; this is a lot of bags.

Abutilons are also nearly perfect shrubs for a shady location, but, unlike the hydrangeas, they can withstand a direct blast of sun during the day without wilting. They broaden the garden palette by blooming primarily in late summer and winter. No other plant in my garden flowers as long—ten months by my count—and it is one of the few plants that grows quickly to its appointed size and then seems to stop. My abutilons grow to a height of about six or eight feet and then remain there, reaching that size in about nine months with the help of lots of water and fertilizer. The best have smallish leaves and large bell-like flowers, and in winter and spring they are smothered with them. Look around and you'll find all sorts of colors, shading from yellow into red with a warm apricot in between, and a pretty white that sparkles in the shade.

Another champion shrub for the shade—even deep shade—is the dark, glossy-green Japanese aucuba. The gold-splattered variegated varieties are the most popular but I have always found them difficult to grow; not so the plain green *Serratifolia*. Aucubas are as slow as a freight train, so don't expect a big shrub for many years.

If you need one more big shrub to round out your shade planting, try *Pittosporum tobira* 'Variegata,' a two-

toned shrub that is tough as nails; in two years it will grow to six feet across and can grow to fifteen feet. It doesn't grow very tall, however, and pruning can keep the shrub smaller. The cream-splashed leaves look as if shafts of sunlight were striking through the shade. 'Wheeler's Dwarf' is a green-leaved pittosporum that also does well in the shade, growing to about six or eight feet across, but only four or five feet tall.

HEDGES, FENCES, AND WALLS

Hedges are one way to build a background and create privacy without taking up too much space. All too often, however, they are a solution to quite another problem—a plant that has grown too large for its space. These mutilated plants do not add to a garden; instead of a leafy wall of green, you see cut and ragged leaves, stubs of branches, and lots of dead, twiggy wood. Some shrubs simply do not like being sheared.

To make a good hedge, a plant must have smallish leaves. Large hedges in the background can have medium-sized leaves (three inches long); hedges in the foreground must have small leaves (an inch long) or you will see too

many cut leaves and the brown scars that appear as the leaf heals. A shrub to be used as a hedge must also grow slowly or you will never stay ahead of the shearing. Even then, the plant must be pruned before it makes more than a few inches of new growth or the older leaves will be shaded by the new and will die out. At that point, it is too late to prune the hedge back to its original size. Even with frequent shearing, a hedge is slowly going to get larger with age, so be sure to allow it a little room to spread. Hedges often lose their lower leaves in time because the growth above shades them, but you can avoid this by pruning on an angle—even a slight angle—so the base of the hedge is always wider than the top and thus receives enough light.

A good hedge can create real drama in the garden if you play with it a little. Leave a passage through it, cut windows in it, add architectural elements—an arched top or finials, perhaps. Hedges and other clipped forms can contrast sharply with more casual plantings, to create special places or focal points in the garden.

Fences, the Ultimate Space-savers, But... Fences and masonry walls are the ultimate space-savers, but they

work best if they are softened by plantings in front of or behind them. Plantings in back of a fence or wall tend to suggest that the enclosed area is only a part of the garden and that there is more beyond the wall. Or take another tack and try to make the fence or wall disappear. Designers often paint fences and walls a shade of deep green or gray green so they blend with the shrubbery planted in front of them. Fences and walls intended to be an unobtrusive background should be as plain as possible.

A fence can be a divider, separating parts of the garden. Dividing a garden with hedges or fences sometimes makes it seem more expansive, since there are other places to go.

Leave Gaps All fences should be built to let air pass through them—the advantage they have over solid walls. Even narrow slits between the boards will allow for air circulation, which makes the garden pleasanter to be in for plants and people. Spaces between the boards also help relieve the pressure of a strong wind and reduce the chance of odd currents and eddies that occur when winds are high. Most city dwellers notice that there are great gusts of wind at the base of tall buildings; a similar phenomenon occurs behind fences—an intensifying of the wind—unless there are gaps that let some of the wind through.

DON'T FORGET VINES

Vines strike some people as being just a little scary and it is easy to see why. Some vines are house-gobblers, tree-totalers, and fence-wreckers. Turn your back on them and they are out of control. They have been known to grow into an attic, to cover windows completely, to rip off shingles. They can even smother a tree. Undoing their damage is hard and heavy work; extricating their victims from the tentacles painfully slow.

But vines have their place. It's the surest way to make a fence attractive or to cover the walls of a house where there is no room for anything wider. Vines can be two-dimensional plants. Because they have no natural shape, they bring a casual air to a garden, a random note. In Mediterranean gardens vines are often trained up into olive trees and other open trees. Only certain vines will do: they must be spare themselves, not too lush, and have a graceful airiness so they are like trimmings on a Christmas tree.

Some of the most commonly used vines are not well-behaved. I would think twice about planting any ivy, even Boston ivy. I have spent weeks trying to remove Algerian ivy from a fence only to discover that the fence had rotted. The builder of my house spent little to embellish the back, so I covered it with Boston ivy, which grows in shade and clings to anything with its little suckerlike pads. Though it makes a handsome green background for the garden, keeping it off the window screens is a monotonous task.

Beware of Wisteria and Other Vines I would be careful about using wisteria, which starts out sweetly enough but in time becomes a monstrous and extremely heavy vine. I am convinced it could cover an entire acre given the chance. If you want those wistful, grapelike flowers, be prepared to prune hard, and often. I would not give a creeping fig a hand-hold. This little vine looks so small and innocent in the nursery container, but at maturity its leaves triple in size and it has the grasp of a green giant. Still nursing

my wounds from the curved, sickle-sharp thorns that are designed to pierce and hold, I would never again plant a 'Belle of Portugal' climbing rose, except perhaps to cover a concrete battlement. It is much too large and quite capable of defending itself from gardeners who have only pruning shears in their holster.

All of these vines undoubtedly have a place, but it probably isn't in the average garden. They need too much room and attention.

Certain Vines for Certain Places But not all vines behave so malevolently. There are others that grow to manageable sizes and are the very models of restraint—their discovery by gardeners is overdue. This is especially true in Southern California because we can grow dozens of demure subtropical vines that flower exuberantly. Their usefulness increases each year because they can grow in those spaces, increasingly common, that are too narrow for anything else. Around new or remodeled homes, and in condominium and apartment courtyards, sliver-sized planting strips are the perfect home for a few well-mannered vines. Here are several worthy of consideration:

Currently at the top of my list is *Stephanotis floribunda*, also known as Madagascar jasmine. This vine is subtropical, reputedly growing only in a narrow frost-free band near the coast, though I have it in my garden which is well back from the beach and I am sure I have seen it much further inland; perhaps it was growing under the protection of eaves. It is a well-mannered vine that can grow in sun or complete shade, as I discovered when I removed an aging shelter from my own garden. The stephanotis had been growing in the dark under an alumi-

The wonderfully fragrant Stephanotis floribunda, *a very slow-growing subtropical vine,*
clings to a ready-made redwood trellis, bolted
to a stucco wall.

num roof and suddenly it found itself
growing in full sun against a south-
facing wall. I was prepared to take it
out, but an experienced landscape contractor and friend told me it would
adjust, and it did, without so much as
a yellowed leaf.

Basking in the warmth of the summer sun, the stephanotis began flowering and in short order was covered with
the white, waxy flowers that are often
used in bridal bouquets, each blossom
sweetly fragrant. In the shade it had
bloomed once or twice, and the blossoms were a delight, but in the sun it
completely covered itself with flowers.
It grows to a very restrained eight to
ten feet, but the price you pay for this
restraint is patience. It grows very
slowly. When I gave neighbors some of
it for their new garden, their contractor
looked at it and muttered, "slowest
plant in the world." Like most vines, it
attaches by twining, which means that
a support of some kind is required.

Perhaps my next favorite subtropical
vine goes by the not very glamorous
name of potato vine, not because it
looks anything like a potato but
because it is a *Solanum,* which is in the
potato family. *Solanum jasminoides* is
what I prefer to call it because the
reference to jasmine is more romantic
if not apt. The flowers are white but
not fragrant, and the vine is a little
scraggly, the foliage sparse. I have one
on the front of my house, growing on
two four-by-eight lattice panels. It
grew very quickly to cover these panels, then hardly at all, but it is always
in flower.

Clematis, and there are many kinds,
is another handsome, well-mannered
vine that can be grown just about
anywhere in the country. And there are
more. Keep vines in mind when you
need a plant that will grow in almost no
space at all.

Support Needed It is even easier to
grow vines on fences, the best support
of all being the ubiquitous chain link
fence. One of the best fence-coverers is
Mandevilla 'Alice du Pont.' This subtropical vine grows just large enough to
cover an eight-foot section of chain
link fence. It grows almost as slowly as
the stephanotis, but it flowers much
more. The pure pink flowers begin in
late spring and keep coming through
summer and into fall, completely hiding the foliage. This vine needs sun
but apparently likes its roots in the
shade, which is also said to be true of
stephanotis.

I have found it easiest to construct a
support using ready-made redwood
trellis panels that measure four by
eight feet. The plant tendrils can then
be woven into the lattice, or simply
tied to it. The panels are attached with
screws to eight-foot redwood two-by-
two's, two at either side and one in the
middle, and these are fastened to the
wall. On a wooden wall, they can be
attached with screws; on stucco, the
screws must be driven into plastic
anchors that are inserted into holes
drilled with a masonry bit. These panels can also be attached to ten-foot,
four-by-four posts so they are free-
standing. This last method makes it
easier to paint the wall behind the
trellis, though the other method allows
you to unscrew the whole construction
and tilt it outward. I cannot attest to
the longevity of these panels but I
would guess that they will last at least
ten years.

TREES

We don't often get the chance to plant
a tree—they usually come with the
place—but when we do, the choice
should be carefully considered. Nothing you plant can become such a

monument (even a national treasure) or such a menace.

Trees are not only backgrounds for your garden but for the whole neighborhood. Of course, they have other functions in the garden, but above all they provide height and scale. A tree can so dominate its site that it makes all human endeavors, even the house, look temporary and of passing importance. Standing next to a tree, we do not feel so big ourselves. Some do not find this particularly comfortable while others find it reassuring, so we see certain neighborhoods full of large trees and others that are completely devoid of them. Not everyone wants to be bothered with the work or expense of caring for a large tree, and there is no doubt that trees involve one or the other—or both!

The Choice Choosing a tree is much like screening a candidate for a job.

Rather than compiling a great list to work from, look for a particular tree for the job in mind. Perhaps the two most important points to consider are large surface root systems and brittle branches, both of which can cause serious structural damage to your grounds. Trees with aggressive surface roots, such as evergreen magnolias, are impossible to garden under, and they can make short work of paving; trees with brittle branches are plain dangerous. But a solution can often be found when siting a tree. A magnolia placed in the background, away from paving, sewer lines, and other plantings, is a pleasure to contemplate and one of the most handsome of backdrops. Even trees that tend to let branches fall are not a problem if they have nothing to fall on. Then think of the eventual height and—as important—the spread. Though people shy away from a big tree, there is nothing

more majestic and lasting, and its height is of no dire consequence if it is otherwise well-behaved.

Its Shadow But do think of the tree's shadow. Some trees cast a dense shade under which it is impossible to garden; others barely freckle the ground. A dense tree shouldn't be anywhere near where you hope to garden, or want to sit, but it is perfect off in the background. Consider if it is deciduous or evergreen: there are places for both. Its nature and shadow will determine what you can grow under it. But don't forget that the ground under a tree is also the perfect place for a patio, especially one that is made of permeable paving—something that water can work its way through and that can be redone should the roots play with it.

Messy Trees People talk about how "messy" a tree is, but it is an unavoid-

Trees are the most important plants in the garden, dominating their surroundings, so they should be carefully chosen. In this garden, a California pepper (that actually comes from Peru), with a botanic name that sounds like a sneeze followed by a polite apology, Schinus molle, *commands the front of the house. Nearby companions include giant bird-of-paradise, pygmy date palms, and a crowd of azaleas. All of the other plantings are kept well away from the sensitive base of the tree.*

able attribute because the leaves and flowers are not permanently attached. Some trees drop their leaves all at once and overwhelm the gardener (but then it is finished), while others drop them a few at a time so it is easy to keep up with the work (though you are never done). Certainly, a tree that has flowers or fruit capable of staining the finish on an automobile or sidewalk is not a good choice to plant with its branches overhanging either; but another site would suit it fine.

Large or Small Leaves? The size of the leaves, flowers, and fruit that a tree bears needs to be considered, but again there is no ideal. Small leaves may be perfect for a tree growing above other plants; when dropped, they will simply disappear. But small leaves falling on a lawn can be a chore to rake up. In general, trees and lawns do not get along well. Trees don't like the frequent watering necessary for growing grass, and a lawn doesn't thrive in the tree's shade, so it is better not to plant them together, though gardeners and designers stubbornly do so despite the horticultural consequences.

Some trees drop leaves that are toxic to other plants and this may make it impossible to garden under them. This toxicity may exist to suppress competition, but it could be the perfect characteristic for a tree that will grow where you don't want anything else—over a patio or in a back corner of the prop-

erty, perhaps. Under a eucalyptus, or avocado for instance, you will find few weeds to hoe.

At Your Arboretum There are many factors to ponder when choosing a tree for your property; the worst possible way to go about it is to buy the first one that appeals to you at the nursery. Instead, in your garden diary set up a chart that lists the necessary characteristics, and as you find trees that you like, do your homework and fill it in. It might look like the chart below.

Don't be in a hurry to plant a tree, but don't put it off too long either. Do some research and discover what you need to know, then plant as soon as possible because trees take a long time to achieve maturity. You want to give your tree an early start so it can begin growing. Consider also that as the tree grows, what grows around it will have to be changed because the nearby plants will find themselves in increasing shade. Be especially aware that most fast-growing trees have serious drawbacks, so be wary.

For all these reasons it is better to keep a tree that is already on the property, even if it is not in the ideal place or is not the ideal tree. Save the tree and work around it, redesigning the garden if need be, then there's no need to start from scratch.

Trees No Bigger than a Bush Though they lack arboreal majesty, there are many small trees that may not be large

enough to create an impressive background, but still serve a useful function. Deciduous magnolias, for instance, have the small scale and showy flowers that make a decided contribution to the garden. Using small trees up close in the landscape is another way to add to the garden's depth and drama; placed in front of other trees, or planted in the middle of the garden, they become a strong foreground forcing the background to recede.

Some small trees will grow under taller trees, a sensible arrangement where another tree has grown so tall that it no longer can function as a backdrop, and you can see right under it. Eastern redbuds are an example of this relationship—they are "understory" trees—and one named 'Forest Pansy' is particularly pretty with its burgundy-colored leaves. It will grow under another taller tree that has a fairly open canopy.

Small trees might also be just the ticket for the background of a small garden. Many new small trees are being introduced by arboretums and nurseries because of this increasing demand, but don't overlook some of the shrubs that grow as large as small trees. Many do.

Sometimes the tree you need is already in place, but it is growing as a large, old shrub. In this case, take out the pruning saw and the loppers, and trim off the lower branches to reveal the tree hidden in its bushy shape.

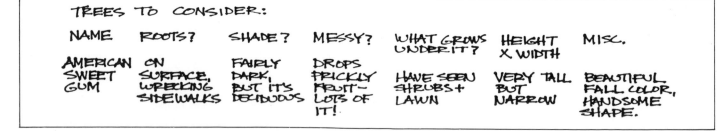

TREES TO CONSIDER:						
NAME	ROOTS?	SHADE?	MESSY?	WHAT GROWS UNDER IT?	HEIGHT X WIDTH	MISC.
AMERICAN SWEET GUM	ON SURFACE, WRECKING SIDEWALKS	FAIRLY DARK, BUT IT'S DECIDUOUS	DROPS PRICKLY FRUIT— LOTS OF IT!	HAVE SEEN SHRUBS + LAWN	VERY TALL BUT NARROW	BEAUTIFUL FALL COLOR, HANDSOME SHAPE.

Plant Portrait

FOSSIL FALL COLOR

About 250 million years ago big changes occurred on this planet. The climate became drier, and the swamps that had nurtured the beginnings of life disappeared gradually. Plants that grew on this soggy ground—bizarre tree-sized horsetails, club mosses, and giant ferns, simple plants that were to become the earth's coal deposits— were replaced by more sophisticated flora. These were the earliest ancestors of modern plant life and, amazingly, two of these prehistoric vegetables somehow survived into

How many garden plants also exist as living fossils? Not many, but here are two: the dawn redwood, an even more ancient ancestor of the already ancient redwood, and the ginkgo, whose spectacular photograph on pages 44–45 opens this chapter. The dawn redwood, pictured on page 80, is the oddest of the pair—a conifer that loses its needles for winter—a deciduous "evergreen."

The ginkgo leaves are living fossils, shown above an actual fossil leaf of a dawn redwood.

modern times, though one almost didn't make it.

For years it was believed that all of the many *Metasequoias*, the first conifers that dominated the ancient forests (even in California) were extinct. But in a discovery that for paleobotanists must have rivaled the finding of a

clutch of dinosaur eggs, a stand of *Metasequoia* was found in 1944 in a remote section of Sichuan, China. Much like California's giant sequoias, these trees were the last of their kind, having been hidden for ages in mist-shrouded mountains, and they were quickly given the popular name of dawn redwood.

Growing side by side (as they do in Southern California's Descanso Gardens), a California redwood and a dawn redwood are difficult to tell apart—until winter. Then the dawn redwood loses its leaves—it is a deciduous conifer, an oddity in the plant world (thus conifer and evergreen are not synonymous). In colder climates the leaves turn a presentable yellow before falling, though in California they turn brown or bronze at best. In compensation, the new spring foliage is the most brilliant green, as fresh as spring itself. Fortunately for gardeners, dawn redwoods never reach the heights of California redwoods. Though they grow fast at first, a mature specimen of a dawn redwood is not much taller than a liquidambar at about eighty feet, and they are naturally narrow.

Our other fossil tree, which was also preserved in China, is the ginkgo. It is almost a conifer, but its large flat leaves place it in its own family, *Ginkgoaceae*, of which it is the sole surviving member. Thought to be extinct in the wild, it apparently has survived in ancient temple gardens. Though the ginkgo is kin to the conifers, its seeds are not housed in cones but are inside plum-like fruits that can be quite odiferous once they fall to the ground. As a result, most ginkgoes are grafted male trees that don't produce fruit. Despite the unpleasant smell of the fruit, the seeds inside are a traditional ingredient in several Oriental dishes,

including a Japanese mustard called *Chawan Mushi*.

Ginkgoes are among the most reliable sources of fall color; the leaves turn a clear, brilliant yellow and make a golden carpet that lasts on the ground for weeks after the tree has become bare. It is such a pretty sight that one ginkgo fancier gives his gardener a vacation so the leaves can lie undisturbed in all their golden glory on the bright green lawn. Press a leaf between the pages of a telephone book and the leaf will retain its color for years.

The ginkgo is an excellent garden tree, tolerant of just about anything, though it is painfully slow to get started and appears to grow only inches the first few years, looking awkward all the time. Gardens would probably be full of ginkgoes if the trees didn't require such patience in their first years on the part of their keepers. In time, ginkgoes become tall, slightly spreading trees, and no tree grows more elegant with age. Most attain a height of about forty feet, but some can grow even taller. There is also a stiffly upright variety named 'Fairmount' that is a good candidate to fill those tight places in a garden, and the variety named 'Autumn Gold' is distinguished by its molten color.

Ginkgoes and dawn redwoods are both excellent lawn trees, tolerating—even appreciating—the constant moisture necessary for the grasses that grow at their feet. Cool-season grasses are probably the best choice for lawns under these trees since they will do much of their growing while the trees are leafless and will appreciate the protection from the hot summer sun. I am probably not going too far out on a limb when I say that there are no better trees for a lawn, and, to top it off, these two have 250 million years of service behind them.

CHAPTER

4

FLOWER BEDS
AND
BORDERS

THE CENTER OF ATTENTION

At different times, different elements have been the center of interest in a garden. In Renaissance Italy, sculpture lined the garden paths and terminated every vista. In Moorish Spain, watercourses followed the paths or were channeled down their center, and splashing fountains or quiet pools were the main focus. In Tudor England, intricate knot gardens were the rage, while landscape designers of a later age used broad sweeps of lawn to capture attention. Finally, at the turn of this century, flowers got their turn.

Flowers have always been a part of gardens, but only in the more humble creations of the Italian peasants, Spanish campesinos, or English country people did flowers take center stage. It was the charm of that rustic creation, the English cottage garden, that influenced innovative gardeners such as William Robinson and Gertrude Jekyll to try flowers on a grander scale in breathtaking borders on large estates.

Pick and Choose Today's garden planner is free to pick and choose from all of these elements, but with flowers growing less and less abundantly in the natural landscape, they are bound to become more precious inside the garden's boundaries. Flowers are without question one of nature's most delightful creations, and their colorful presence is increasingly treasured.

There are other good reasons to make flowers important in a garden. Gazebos, patios, swimming pools, spas, and other man-made elements may be central to the design of a garden, but these creations are short-lived as attention-getters. One look usually suffices. Flowers, on the other hand, change with each hour, each season. They come in every con-

ceivable color and texture, and the possibilities of how and where they might be used are limitless. They can be planted and replanted, dug up and moved around, mixed and matched. One can never see all there is to see or learn all there is to know about flowers; since there is always something new to search for and acquire, the shopper in all of us can be satisfied.

Not everyone shares this affinity for flowers. Some want nothing to do with the hard work; some find flowers untidy and would prefer neat paving, a pool, or perhaps a lawn where something large and more exciting could be grown—trees or shrubbery. But this is what separates true gardeners from people who own a piece of land: Gardeners are those who believe that a garden without flowers is simply a yard. This does not mean that the other garden elements need be ignored or tucked away in some forgotten corner, only that they should be secondary to the play of nature. Water in a garden is certainly as decorative today as it was in Moorish times, and sculpture can look very much at home, but flowers will prove to be a more satisfying center of attention for a gardener or for anyone who longs for an antidote to the hectic life that is bustling just outside the garden walls.

Where We Are and Where They Might Be At this point in our planning we have carefully orchestrated the rest of the garden so the eye has a path to follow and that path leads to the flower beds, though not necessarily in a straight line. Flower beds or borders can be placed almost anywhere, but in your planning you are bound to discover that some places are better than others.

If you have mapped the hourly movement of shadows across your gar-

While there are many interesting and dramatic things that could be the center of attention in a garden, the most satisfying is a bed of flowers. White 'Iceberg' roses are the anchors in the bed on pages 82–83 and 84. Roses ought to be in every flower bed because they are in bloom for so much of the year, but there are other plants that glorify this garden, including a cloud of the tiny cream flowers of coral bells, lavender, and rosemary, dianthus, and a low-growing pink sun rose. The entry is framed by Solanum jasminoides, and the path is flanked by compact eugenias.

This is how big a flower bed ought to be, allowing plenty of room for a great variety—different heights, textures, and colors. It is nine feet deep, with a narrow work path just against the fence behind it, allowing access from the back. Growing here are bulbs, annuals, perennials, roses (mostly miniatures), and even a few vegetables.

den, you now know where the sunniest spots are. Following the advice in chapter three, you have created a background against which flowers can be viewed. You should also have a pretty good idea of where you are going to be sitting in your garden or where you are most likely to be when viewing it. With any luck at all, you should now be able to point with assurance to particular spots on your plans or models and say, "that's where the flowers are going to look best and grow best."

THE BIG BED

What this garden bed has that others do not is room to grow flowers—many flowers. There is sufficient space to hold a great variety—annuals and bulbs in their season, perennials, even small shrubs such as roses and azaleas, grown mostly for their flowers. Size and scale produce drama not found in smaller plots. The depth of the large bed gives the drama a chance to build, with smaller spreading plants in the foreground framed by taller and taller plants toward the back, one showcasing the other in theater-like staging.

Nine Feet It's a common mistake, not allowing enough room for flowers, but one that can easily be avoided or remedied. The typical suburban flower bed is about three feet deep, but the one pictured here is three times that size—nine ample feet between the path and the fence just for flowers. And this is not an especially large yard; its owner simply has dedicated more of it to flowers.

If there is a familiar look to this garden bed, it is owing to its English heritage, for it was in England that grand borders were first used. This is not the traditional English herbaceous

border, however, but a casual California equivalent. It relies heavily on a strong backbone of perennial plants (it's nice about these more permanent plantings that they keep the stage from looking too empty between the major acts), but it also makes use of seasonal bulbs and annuals, replanted in fall or spring, then pulled out at season's end.

If a composition as complicated as this looks hopeless for an amateur gardener, realize that this big bed was not planted all at once but evolved slowly, with plants and flowers going in as they were discovered at nurseries or at neighbors (many of them were started as divisions or cuttings from other gardens). There is always a necessary awkward period during which one discovers that this doesn't go with that—or when plants grow taller, wider, or shorter than anticipated—but constant fiddling and readjustment is part of the gardening process.

Hoick Them Out Victoria Sackville-West, who popularized informal flower borders on a grand scale at Sissinghurst, England, said, "Gardening is largely a question of mixing one sort of plant with another sort of plant, and of seeing how they marry happily together; and if you see that they don't marry happily together, then you must hoick one of them out and be quite ruthless about it. That is the only way to garden."

If that sounds like a lot of work, it is, but all that yanking out does not happen all at once as it does with beds of annuals or mass plantings of bulbs. Rather, it requires regular care—a little here and a little there; this is a garden to putter in.

When the weather is nice there is always something to do in a large flower bed, with room to try something new. You can even let things slide a bit;

Here is another big bed with a tremendous variety of plants, lower in profile to show the stone wall behind them. The wall is topped by climbing roses, two old varieties, 'Lady Forteviat' and 'Inspiration.' Clumps of daylilies and bearded iris are the anchors in this bed; perennials include columbine, coral bells, English daisy, and candytuft. Among the annuals are nasturtiums, lobelia, Iceland poppies, and also a great many bulbs.

plants past their prime, or even a few weeds, will hardly be noticed in the crowd, and other plants will draw the eye away or hide the offenders' untidiness. This is a definite advantage of a bed that is large enough to hold a great variety.

Room for Everybody In a big bed there's room for everybody, and this variety of plants is the fun of it. Freshly opened flowers greet you every morning, with always a surprise in store—colors that are unusually good together, or textures that seem just right; something blooming that you had forgotten about or something flowering for the first time. As with life in a big family, there is never a dull moment.

HOW BIG IS BIG ENOUGH?

One is tempted to say that flower beds or borders can't be too big, but there are limits, one being how far you can reach. The average person can just grab hold of a weed three feet away from where he is kneeling, and that's probably why the typical garden bed is only three feet wide. But you can easily step a little way into the front of a garden bed because the plants growing there are low enough to allow it, so now the bed can be six feet wide. If you are concerned that stepping into the bed will ruin your shoes, or worse yet, compact the soil, try putting flat stones or small pavers here and there in the front of the flower bed, giving you places to step.

You can also reach the bed from the back, for behind many large borders there is another small path for access. It is usually unseen because the flowers in front of it hide it completely, but they're not so tall that they prevent your stepping into the bed from the

back. So now you can reach six feet from front and three from the back, and your garden bed can be nine feet across. A nine-foot-wide bed is a nice size to shoot for, with an extra foot or so in back for that access path. Nine feet allows you to grow several three-foot-wide plants from front to back, enough to build some drama.

Three-foot Plants Conveniently, many flowering plants—perennials and roses in particular—grow to be about three feet across, and this is where many gardeners get in trouble. A dainty dianthus looks full and bushy in a gallon nursery can when it is only a foot across, but a few years later it will have easily spread to three feet in width. When you plant it, be sure to allow room for lateral growth.

Most annual flowers and bulbs are considerably smaller than perennials and they can be used in the foreground of a flower bed to add even more variety. They tend to look better planted in groups that seem about the right size when they measure three feet across. Be forewarned that when a bed is big and the flowers are spaced with room for future expansion, it is going to look pretty empty at first. Here is where annual flowers and some bulbs can help, temporarily filling the spaces until the perennials and more shrubby flowers fill out and fill in.

Another Trick Empty ground is nothing to be ashamed of and, in fact, it is necessary while you are waiting for plants to grow. Most gardeners like to avoid seeing these garden "bald spots," so here's another trick: Design the garden beds so they are usually viewed from a slight distance. In other words, don't put them directly below where you are to be standing or right next to where you and your visitors sit. This

way you will not be looking down on the beds, nor staring at the bare ground that is inevitably between plants. Instead, you will be looking across the bed, with plants screening the spots of bare earth. Weeds and plants' untidy parts will also be less noticeable so their presence will not disturb your enjoyment of the garden —you will not feel compelled to jump up and take care of them this instant or to plant more, when you should be happily anticipating the plants that will soon be filling in.

THINK OF FOLIAGE FIRST, BUT BEGIN WITH ROSES

When you start to plan a flower bed, one way to begin is with roses. Roses are often planted off by themselves, but they are an almost perfect anchor for a mixed flower bed. Modern roses flower often, more often than just about any other plant, so even when other flowers are not in bloom, roses are likely to be. Furthermore, you can find roses in a variety of of colors: reds, pinks, yellows, or oranges, so they will

fit into any color scheme.

However, there is a trade-off when you plant roses in a bed of other flowers—the roses won't grow as big as they do when planted by themselves. (This could be seen as an advantage in California where roses sometimes grow too tall to show well.) Because of the competition from other plants, there will be fewer rose flowers and they will be slightly smaller, but most gardeners will hardly notice this decrease in performance.

Planning a flower bed that will

include roses gives you a good opportunity to use the rule of three's and five's. Make a drawing of the bed and draw circles indicating where roses might go. Give each bush at least three feet of space and place the rose bushes about three feet back from the edge of the bed so you can plant other flowers in front of them. Don't set them too far into the bed or you won't be able to reach the plants easily, and roses need frequent care, such as cutting off dead flowers.

Roses also work well as anchors because they have handsome foliage.

Foliage as Important as Flowers A plant's foliage—in the case of roses, glossy burgundy leaves that change to dark green as they mature—is as important as its flowers; when there are no flowers, the foliage must carry the show. Modern English gardeners are especially expert at using foliage in a flower bed. Look at their gardens and note how different kinds of leaves play an important role. Plants with large leaves and plants with small ones are used, as well as burgundy-colored leaves, leaves streaked with gold, and frequently subtle gray or silver foliage. Study photos of fine English gardens and you will see the masterful use of fine textures—the ferny foliage of yarrow, for instance—and of coarse textures—the leaves of cardoon or acanthus. English gardeners are very fond of spiky leaves.

Too often flower beds rely mostly on flower color, while the foliage is a uniform green, frequently with leaves or similar sizes and textures. Beds of annuals are particularly prone to this leafy blandness since most have foliage colored a medium green.

Time to Go Window Shopping The only way to find out what the possibilities

really are is to do a little window shopping at nurseries. Look for interesting foliage. Perhaps buy a few plants, take them home, and begin experimenting. Arrange them (still in their nursery cans), rearrange them, and see what you like. Be bold and try groups that you might not normally consider. If your local nursery doesn't have much variety, try another, or ask a good gardener where he buys his plants. There are many specialty nurseries, most of them backyard businesses, that carry unusual plants. You will find that just a few extraordinary plants can bring excitement and life to the design of a garden bed.

THANK GOODNESS FOR PERENNIALS

When you begin looking for plants that will add interest to your flower bed, you will soon find yourself saying, "Thank goodness for perennials." What's so special about perennials? The great thing they offer is variety—there is no end to their numbers, no color they don't come in, no limitation on size or shape. As an added advantage, they will grow in your garden for quite a while. You can't plant them and forget them, but you can count on their lasting several years without much attention other than keeping up with the weeding, watering, and, on occasion, a little tidying up.

Sophisticates With perennials you can make a more sophisticated and somewhat more subtle composition. Instead of replanting the whole garden every six months, you can add to it, subtract when necessary, or move things about. It is easy to move perennials; in fact, a change of locale is required after a few years. Most perennials are not as brilliantly colored as annuals (annuals must be seen by bees if they are to be pollinated and make seed for survival for another year, so they wear the wildest outfits). Perennials are just dressed in foliage for much of the year. For compensation, many perennials have beautiful foliage, which few annuals can boast of. Some are even grown just for their foliage, such as the silvery lamb's ears or the bronze ajuga.

Herbaceous and Other Perennials The traditional perennial is the herbaceous perennial—it dies completely to the ground every winter, or nearly so, springing back from the roots the following year. In California and in other Sunbelt gardens, we grow many plants that are called perennials but that are technically something else. Many are actually "subshrubs," if you look them up in a botanical reference book—short-lived, smallish shrubs. Some of these do not go dormant but actually bloom in the dead of winter. Some perennials, such as delphiniums in California, are grown as if they were annuals—you plant them each year and pull them out at the end of their season. In general, another benefit of adding perennials to a flower border is that they lengthen the flowering season, especially in mild climates.

Not Really Hard to Grow Many perennials are easy to grow, actually easier than annuals, although some require a bit of gardening skill. They often differ remarkably in their culture, but learning how to grow them is perhaps the most satisfying part of the adventure. But don't let it scare you away. A lot of gardeners have been intimidated by phrases such as "when to cut back" or "how to divide," but these techniques can be learned simply by trial and error—most perennials are very forgiving.

Perennials such as the tall blue delphiniums, the yellow and red columbine, the deep red coral bells, and the soft magenta nicotiana are important elements of this flower bed, not simply for their brilliance of color, but because they add a variety of heights and textures. A white 'Iceberg' rose also grows here with an assortment of annuals that includes stock and Iceland poppies. The tall foxgloves in the background are neither annuals nor perennials; they are biennials, growing one year, blooming the next, then dying. But in California, they grow and flower in just one season.

Plant Portrait

THE DAINTY DIANTHUS

Garden pinks, or dianthus, are the baby sisters of the carnation clan. They have the delicate ruffled beauty and delightful scent of carnations, but their flowers are simpler and they are on shorter stems (six to ten inches) that do not need staking to stay upright. Pinks and carnations are botanically *Dianthus* and are "perhaps native to the Mediterranean region," according to the best authorities. That's a good guess, because they do have the gray foliage of plants accustomed to a lot of sun. It may even be the best guess, because pinks have been grown in gardens since antiquity, and their true origins are hidden in the haze of the past.

If there were garden "ancient worthies," dianthus would be included in their ranks. They are ancient indeed, having adorned garlands and coronets in Greece and Rome, survived the Middle Ages in cloistered monastery gardens where their flowers flavored wines and graced illuminated manuscripts, and were transported to England, either by Norman monks or possibly attached to the stones that were imported for Norman watchtowers (depending on which account you read).

As early as 1578, an herbal distinguished between "coronations" and the "small feathered Gillofers, known as Pynkes, Soppes-in-wine, and small Honesties." In Shakespeare's time, the smaller dianthus was commonly called gillyflower, and before that, Chaucer knew it as "gilofre," until pink became the popular name.

They became popular flowers in Elizabethan times and, later, at their zenith, several hundred varieties of pinks and carnations were offered by English nurseries, though few of those

made it to our own shores. Because the best kinds must be grown from cuttings, they were difficult to import because of strict plant quarantines, but enough did emigrate to brighten our gardens with their dainty flowers and silvery foliage.

History alone gives them charm.

with blossoms in April and May. In summer, the plants are a low mound of gray, but by fall some of the leaves turn brown and the plants are less than tidy. Shearing flowering stems as they fade in summer helps encourage new growth and may prompt them to flower again. No need to be too careful—just get out the hedge shears, cut off the old flower stalks, and don't worry if you trim a little off the leaves.

Different varieties of dianthus are surprisingly different horticulturally as well. I have grown a variety called Penny that blooms all year and seems likely to live forever. It is now five years old and is a four-foot-wide patch of gray in the garden, usually covered with flowers. Other varieties I have tried are not nearly as long-lived and tend to flower at certain definite times. I will take a guess and say that the simpler the flower—those with single rather than double petals—the sturdier the plant. But most are not what I would call permanent plants in the garden, eventually dying out in sections, so I always keep a few cuttings going to make sure I don't lose them.

In England, they have naturalized on lofty castle walls, which hints at their soil preference—gritty or porous with the speediest of drainage. But this doesn't mean they like drought. On the contrary, they seem to need as much water as any other plant; they just don't want to sit in puddles of it.

Dianthus are started anew from "slips" (a garden word that existed in Shakespeare's time)—short shoots that do not terminate in a flower or bud. These should be gently pulled off the plant so that a small "heel" of the parent stem remains, then rooted in damp sand. The shoots are easy to root; simply strip off some of the lower leaves, plunge them partway into pure sand, and keep moist.

Their scent is heavenly, and the gray foliage offers welcome relief in a too-green garden. Low and sturdy, they make an elegant, nearly perfect, edge for a flower border and are especially attractive next to paths, spreading onto the pavement.

Dianthus make a delightful addition to the late spring and summer garden, where they thrive in a sunny spot, although they may be difficult at other times of the year. Typically, they grow wonderfully the first year, spreading into a dense, gray mound several inches high and a foot or two across, then in California covering themselves

Garden Visit

ONE BIG BORDER

In many respects it would be difficult to find a less typical California garden than the one pictured here. True, there is a swimming pool and a patio, but this garden is devoted to plants not to outdoor living, as are so many gardens in this sunny climate.

It is the garden of Ruth Borun, an avid gardener who was not too proud to call in a little help when faced with bringing order to her burgeoning collection of remarkable plants. Like many a gardener's garden, it had grown joyfully but haphazardly over the years. Garden designer Chris Rosmini was asked to help with its reorganization; the huge raised bed that sweeps the length of the garden was her solution.

The bed is so broad that there has to be a path behind it, without which the plants in the center would be completely out of reach. As it is, one must step gingerly through the lush growth to reach the remote interior. It is wide enough to hold a great variety of plants. Though most are perennials of one kind or another, the most obvious exceptions at this time of the year are the watsonias, annuals whose tall pink and white bulbs are in bloom. This bed is wide enough to accommodate truly tall plants. Near the pool you can see a profusion of perennials grown mostly for their foliage, especially those with gray leaves. This rich array entices you to spend a great deal of time looking at the plantings—this is what most pleases avid gardeners.

The work that went into the Borun border was phenomenal. Ruth Borun is always stopping to pull this weed or nip that bud. That is what gardening is all about and yet another reason why perennials are so popular with people who love to grow things.

There is ample room for really big flowers in this curving raised bed that borders a lawn on one side and has a path on the other for easy access. The tallest plants are watsonias, South African bulbs that are completely at home in this Los Angeles garden. Columbines and penstemon also stand tall, while Verbena rigida stand out—they are the pure purple flowers in the foreground. Tufts of blue fescue, an ornamental grass, can be seen in the front row, perched atop the wall of broken concrete.

DIVISION AND DORMANCY

In time, most true perennials need to be cut back and divided. They originated in cooler climates, where they had to die to the ground to survive winter. In the garden, we cut them back instead, because it's neater and in mild climates, like California's, we need to force them to rest. The champion tool for cutting back perennials is actually made for edging the lawn—the Corona No. 5 shear—long and hefty enough to cut a bunch of stems at once.

Be aware that not all perennials sold as such should be cut back to the ground. Remember that some are not true herbaceous perennials and they should usually just be tidied up. If you're in doubt, leave the plant alone and see if the stems die back or not. If a perennial flowers early in the season, cut it back then and it may flower again. Later in the season, hold off until the onset of winter and enjoy the seed stalks produced after the flowers.

Ideally, in California's mild climate, you will never have a garden of perennials that are all cut back and dormant. There are plenty of plants sold as perennials that look good at all times of the year. But there is a definite down time in November and December when there are few or no flowers and many plants are producing only seed stalks. This is the time of year to "rework the border," which usually means digging and dividing.

Simple Division Division is necessary because most true perennials grow as spreading clumps. If you look closely at a true perennial, you will see that what appears to be one plant is actually a number of smaller plants growing together. As they grow ever wider, they deplete the soil beneath them so totally that the center of the clump begins to fail. At this point, dig it up and either pull the clump apart or slice it apart with a sharp spade. Most serious perennial gardeners keep a flat-bladed spade, sharpened with a coarse file, just for this purpose.

Dig the entire clump out of the ground so you can see what you're dealing with and then split it apart. These clumps can get pretty heavy, so this might not be feasible if yours has grown very large—one reason you want to attend to this every few years. The old center of the clump is usually discarded, and the vigorous younger outer growth divided into small pieces and replanted. Extra divisions can be given away and most gardeners get pretty shrewd about swapping their extras for some perennial they don't have. Most of this dividing (and swapping) is done during winter.

Renew the Soil Because perennials use a soil so heavily, it is very important to prepare the soil thoroughly before planting. The idea is to make it as rich as possible by adding fertilizer and organic amendments (the kind sold by the bag at nurseries—usually a mix of specially treated barks and sawdust). These are mixed in with a spade, spading fork, or tiller, and the result is a fluffy, rich soil that will sustain a perennial for a number of years. When it is time to dig and divide, the soil can be renewed by adding still more organic material, especially fertilizer. Any complete granular fertilizer will do.

A well-prepared soil is also a lot easier to dig in, so the perennials are easier to dig up, divide, or move. This is one advantage of using perennials. If you don't like the way they look where they are growing, or if they grow too tall or wide for their spot, it is no big problem to move them elsewhere.

Dividing perennials is not the mystery it is often made out to be. Very simply, many perennials grow as clumps of individual plants and in time the inside of the clump deteriorates. Then the idea is to dig it from the soil, split the clump apart, discard the old center and replant the fresh outer growth. Two examples are pictured here. A big clump of agapanthus at the upper left and right, and a clump of a classic herbaceous perennial, veronica, at the lower left and right. Note the individual plants of the veronica—one stem with roots.

Garden Visit

GRANDSTAND GARDENING

There is something to be said for grandstanding in the garden—arranging all of the plants with the shortest in front, the tallest in back and the in-betweens in between, as if all the flowers were sitting neatly on bleachers. This classic arrangement still gets the most applause, especially when the flowers are in the front yard, as the two borders pictured here happen to be. Barely a leaf or stem is visible, with the shorter plants hiding all the foliage of the others, so only the flowers can be seen.

Notice the other classic staging devices used in these two beds. Wisely, they have been set back a little from the street or sidewalk. This not only keeps the flowers from being trampled, but it allows that narrow strip of lawn between street and garden to make a nice green foreground for the colorful blooms. At the same time, it prevents the glare of the adjacent concrete from intruding. If the sidewalk were a more handsome or elegant path in the back of the garden, this strip of lawn wouldn't be necessary. There are good reasons not to have it, but instead to

The two summer gardens on these pages are striking examples of bleacher-like staging. White vinca and perennial candytuft (not yet in bloom) comprise the lowest front row in the garden on page 98. Behind them come marigolds and marguerites, spikes of purple salvia. Taller zinnias and roses occupy the back.

Lobelia and sweet alyssum have front-row seats. Pink and red annual phlox, pansies, and Chrysanthemum paludosum are behind them, with zinnias in back. Overlooking all is still another row, of roses.

let the flowers spill over into the strip. However, necessity sometimes forces compromises in the garden plan. Backing up the flowers are substantial walls of brick or stone—natural materials that complement the flowers. They complete the picture, acting as one side of the frame, the lawn being the other.

The beds are not too narrow; one is about five feet broad, the other has undulations that vary from four to eight feet. To grandstand like this requires a variety of heights and a wide enough area. Both beds are filled with summer flowers. Zinnias are the major players, but perhaps more important are the smaller flowers in the foregrounds since they are the very foundations of the planting compositions and must look the tidiest. In one bed, a low hedge of perennial candytuft, *Iberis* (out of flower at the time of the photograph), does the job year round. In the other bed the front row is occupied by old-reliable sweet alyssum and lobelia in two shades, a dark violet and a lighter lavender. These spill right onto the lawn, so the grass must be edged by hand.

The second row has two tiny chrysanthemums, neither of which has a proper common name: *Chrysanthemum paludosum* has white blooms that look like Shasta daisies, and the *C. multicaule* has buttery-yellow flowers, partially closed on this overcast day. Perennials of various sorts, including the blue bedder *Salvia farinacea*, dwarf agapanthus, and even an ice plant also grow there. In the other bed, summer's favorite annual, miscalled *Vinca rosea* (it's really *Catharanthus*) provides a cooling white influence.

Note that both garden beds use roses at the very back of the borders, where you can see their flowers but not their scraggly bases—a neat trick.

Annuals have the brightest and splashiest colors of all, zinnias being the perfect example. The strain called California Giants on page 100 is one of the best and most vivid.

Mary Ellen Guffey, pictured on page 101, tends a garden planted mostly with annuals on a hillside in Malibu. This is the spring garden, put in during the fall, a favorite time to plant in California.

There is no reason not to mix annuals, bulbs, perennials, or any other plant, in the same bed. The spring garden on page 102 by Sassafras Nursery & Landscaping uses yellow tulips and a pink double tulip named 'Angelique' with anemones, cineraria, primroses and forget-me-nots, all happy under the light shade of an old olive.

A PLACE FOR ANNUALS

Though perennial flowers offer more variety and more interesting foliage, annual flowers such as zinnias and marigolds are by far the brightest and the most floriferous. Every garden, including the most subdued, should have a place for them, even if it is only in pots. True annuals grow, flower, and die in the course of a single year. This probably accounts for their flamboyant colors and huge flowers—they have only a short time in which to attract bees and other pollinators if their race is to survive into another year.

Many of the most colorful annuals originated in Mexico—zinnias and marigolds are among the best known—and they flower during the warmest weather in sunny colors. They are native to an area in Mexico where win-

ters are so dry that most plants cannot survive the season, so these annuals die in winter. Summers are, by contrast, wet and warm, and this is when they sprout and grow. In California, we call these the warm-season annuals, because they are planted in spring for summer bloom.

The Cool-Season Crop We also grow annuals that come from climates much like California's (some do come from this state, including California poppies and godetia or farewell-to-spring). In these climates, the summers are dry but the winters are wet, so these flowers grow during the cool, rainy season and we call them cool-season annuals. In other parts of the country, these cool-season annuals are usually planted very early in spring, before those that need warmer weather. Most

of these cool-season annuals can tolerate a little frost.

Interestingly, these annuals tend also to have cooler colors, though there are some very bright exceptions. Canterbury bells, cineraria, English daisy, foxglove, larkspur, linaria, and stock are some cool-season annuals (or plants grown like annuals) with cool colors; calendulas, iceland poppies, and pansies are some with much warmer colors.

Not Actually Annuals Some plants grown as annuals actually aren't. They may be biennials (such as Canterbury bells or foxglove) or perennials (such as English daisies), but through the years gardeners have discovered that these plants are most successful when planted every year, then taken out at the end of their season. In Southern California, the popular impatiens will last more than a year, but they look their best if they are replanted every spring.

Bays, Plots, and Pots If you use shrubs and perennials to form the backbone of your flower bed, create some bays in which to plant the annuals. Most annuals are fairly short-stemmed compared to perennials, so little bays cut out of the front edge of the flower bed make perfect homes for them.

To the very sensitive perfectionist, the strong colors of many annuals are inharmonious with the more muted colors of perennials. If this is an objection, try planting annuals in their own little plots in another part of the garden. You might even plant your annuals in beds in the front yard and perennials in the back to make the best of both worlds. Or plant some of the vivid annuals in pots. Annuals do particularly well in containers because they grow fast, can take a lot of water, and thrive on fertilizer. Pots filled with bright annuals bring color close to the sides of the house where patios or paving preclude planting in the ground.

That Summer Sun-Winter Shade Problem Annuals are also a solution for that summer sun-winter shade problem. There are parts of the garden that get drenched in sunlight in summer, but are bathed in shade all winter when the shadows lengthen. In winter, use cool-season flowers such as primroses or cinerarias that tolerate shade, replanting these beds in spring to give the garden summer color with those flowers that like the sun.

Plant Portrait

PANSIES IN PARTICULAR

The most enduring and perhaps endearing of fall-planted, cool-season flowers are the pansies and violas, pansies being the flowers with the charming, contrasting faces, and violas the ones that are plain-faced but just as pretty.

In California, if they are planted in October they will flower within weeks and keep on flowering until the first hot days of summer, maybe longer. Even if they get straggly after a few months, there is a way to bring them back. And if you are one of the unlucky few who have had pansies die suddenly for no apparent reason, there is a solution for this as well.

Pansies have been an important part of California gardening for a long time. In 1908 John McLaren, creator of San Francisco's Golden Gate Park and author of one of the earliest books on California gardening, said of the pansy: "This popular plant is a favorite of rich and poor alike, everyone who has a garden growing a few pansies. This is deservedly so, in view of its wonderful variety of color and its free-flowering habit together with the ease with which it may be grown."

At that time, much attention was being given to hybridizing and crossing, with the goal being bigger and bigger flowers. In 1915, E. J. Wickson noted in *California Garden Flowers:* "Pansies are a great delight if well grown from choice strains of seed, of which a number of seedsmen are making a specialty. A pansy specialist is coming to be regarded as a very high-class horticulturist."

Bigger and Better By 1928 choice strains made the cover of at least one seed catalogue, that of the Los Angeles firm of Aggeleler & Musser, a consider-able feat considering the competition from other flowers and vegetables. These strains had names such as Mammoth Wonder, A&M Super Maximum, and Mastodon, the names indicating that size was of utmost importance. About the same time plants as well as seed began to be sold, but not in plastic pots as they are today. You dug your own from fields and loaded them into wooden boxes. At Paul J. Howard's Flowerland nursery on La Brea, plants were sold for fifty cents a dozen or three dollars per 100. By 1949 Better Gardens nursery in San Marino was offering Genuine Imported Rogglie Swiss Giants, Steele's, and a mix named Santa Anita Jumbo, which shows how far back the tradition of pansies blooming at the Santa Anita racetrack goes.

The culmination of all this breeding was a strain called Majestic Giants which won the first All-America award for pansies. According to Lew Whitney of Roger's Gardens in Corona del Mar, who has planted thousands of these flowers in gardens, they are still the best of the big-flowered, long-stemmed, pretty-faced pansies and the most popular at nurseries.

Those long stems, by the way, were developed so pansies could be cut and arranged, a problem modern gardeners have not had to contend with. Lew remembers his mother having a special shallow bowl just for pansies, and old seed catalogues make quite a point of long-stemmed pansies for cutting. One contemporary seed catalogue from the English firm of Thompson & Morgan still carries two cut-flower strains—Violet Queen and Yellow Queen—and the catalogue photos of these pansies, neatly tied into little bundles, ought to tempt one to try pansies as cut flowers. But for attractive cut flowers you really needn't look further than

Violas and pansies are perfect in pots, especially if the containers are set up on a ledge so you can look into those little flower faces. This bowl is filled with a strain named Beaconsfield.

the Majestic Giants.

There are other strains of large-flowered pansies, and there are even some called Steele's, presumably descended from that old-time strain now valued for their smaller, but softer-colored flowers. There is also a mix called Race Track, which honors the huge field planted every year in the center of the Santa Anita racetrack.

Violas As pendulums have a way of doing, this one is now swinging back and the smaller-flowered violas are returning to fashion. One good reason is that the ancestor of all violas is a perennial, and as a result violas or viola-flowered pansies bloom the longest of the lot. They can even live over from year to year.

Violas are descended from *Viola cornuta*, but so much crossing has gone on that most violas are now a mix of pansy and viola, which is why some seed catalogues invented the term viola-flowered pansies. But you are pretty safe if you call any plain-faced pansy a viola. The best of these is a strain called Crystal Bowl, which is the common plain-faced pansy at nurseries, sold either as a mix or as separate colors. It is the longest-flowering of its kind, and it blooms for what seems forever. You are likely to tire of it long before it gives up. Clear Crystal is a similar strain. You will also find some other small-flowered violas that are always one color, such as a strain called Ruby or Ruby Queen, whose deep red blooms are more the color of a garnet and are among the most velvety of violas.

Just What Are They? It is a little harder to figure out what to call some of the pansies or violas that fall somewhere between the two categories. One of these is called Bambini, and it has the

cutest of all pansy faces with distinct eyes and a smile but small, viola-sized blossoms. Beaconsfield is an interesting pansy with the three lower petals a deep purple and the uppermost pure white. Moody Blues is striking with the upper petals colored purple and a purple face on the lower white petals. Imperial Blue and Imperial Orange Prince have only faint faces, but they are two of the prettiest violas or pansies, whichever they are.

You may also find some small-flowered pansies or violas that have extremely deep color and complicated markings. These are sold only in small pots, when they are in flower, and they are seldom named, but I suspect that they are descendants of what used to be called Shakespeare's pansies—violas with some Johnny-jump-up in them.

The Johnny-jump-up is the least civilized of the viola clan and grows so easily it will naturalize in gardens. Some even consider it a weed. It has its own botanical name of *Viola tricolor*, a reference to the lilac, purple, and yellow petals. A fancier Johnny-jump-up, which is a deep, velvety purple, is named 'King Henry' two more charming flowers would be hard to find.

This by no means exhausts the list, but it should help with the shopping because the best way to buy pansies or violas—if you want to plant them by the dozens in the ground—is when they are small and compact, well before they have flowered.

Pansy Problems One reader wrote in early spring, "Some of my violas are already giving up the ghost, the stalk seemingly severed right at the soil line." Another, "I lose lots of pansies each year. Have tried everything—putting them on mounds, cutting back watering, more watering, etc. And they

Pansies and violas are a little hard to tell apart; Azure Blue at upper left is a pansy, and Crystal Bowl, just below, is a viola. 'King George' at upper right is a Johnny-jump-up.

still die. Healthy plants seem to just rot away." The problem is a fungus, one of the many named *Rhizoctonia*. It attacks the very base of the plant and literally severs it from the roots. It may be brought on by too much water, but some readers suggested that even cutting down on the watering didn't help.

The solution was suggested by Lew Whitney at Roger's Gardens. They spray the plants with Ortho Multipurpose Fungicide, which contains the active ingredient Daconil, emphasizing that this will not bring back plants already infected, but—in their experience—will prevent the fungus from attacking nearby pansies or violas. It can be used preventively by spraying new plantings as soon as they go into the ground, then following up with a second spraying a few weeks later. The fungus lives only on the soil's surface so there is no need to soak or drench the soil; just get the surface good and wet, especially around the base of the plants.

Cut Them Back All pansies, but in particular the smaller, viola-flowered strains, will bloom from January into early summer. This was known back in Wickson's time, and a report from Mr. W. M. Bristol of San Bernadino, in the 1915 edition of *California Garden Flowers*, states: "Probably there is no place better adapted to the production of magnificent pansies than southern California. The weather from January to July is more or less cool and moist, conditions favorable to the growth of the pansy, and with proper management the plants will produce an immense crop of blossoms of large size."

Since they last such a long time in the garden, it is common for pansies and violas eventually to get long, leggy, and straggly, and you certainly want to avoid buying them when they already look like that. At the nursery, find tight, compact plants that have not begun to lean or topple. Should they become leggy in the ground, try another trick passed along by Lew Whitney. Even though it sounds drastic, cut pansies and violas back to within an inch of the ground; fertilize and water them and watch them come back! If only a few stems become leggy, these can be pinched back. The reason stems become long is most often lack of light. Heed Mr. Bristol's advice from 1915: "Don't believe the threadbare and absurd statement that 'pansies like a shady place.' Set them where they will receive full sun but no reflected heat from buildings."

Not for Shade Though pansies will tolerate some shade, they prefer sun; therefore the information found on some plant labels at a nursery, "plant in part shade or shade," is dead wrong.

"Remove all blossoms as they wilt," continues Mr. Bristol and this advice is seconded by Mr. Whitney. If pansies and violas are allowed to go to seed, they will not last nearly as long as they should. Lew Whitney goes so far as to let his thumbnail grow a little longer in winter so he can use it in true nurseryman fashion to nip off the pansy flowers as they fade.

What pansies and violas like best is a cool and moist soil, so it is worth the effort to add organic amendments before planting and to mulch after planting. Their beds must never be allowed to dry out. These plants like moisture, but Mr. Bristol's advice is again as appropriate today as when he wrote it: "Don't give them a shower-bath with the hose every day or two. It is folly. It hardens and packs the ground while the roots may be suffering for moisture. Once a week or two make holes or furrows among the plants and keep water therein until the ground is thoroughly soaked."

You may not want to irrigate with furrows, but when you water, do so thoroughly. Old books make quite a point of never letting pansies go completely dry and of mulching with some organic material. Full sun for the tops, cool and moist for the roots.

A Place for Pansies The traditional place to plant pansies has always been along the front walk so their cheery faces can welcome visitors. A plan in the 1908 edition of *California Gardening* shows pansies on either side of the walk and flanking the front door against the house, at the base of the rose bushes. Because they are neat and long-lasting, pansies and violas are among the best choices to plant in the front of the flower bed or the front row of a perennial border.

Pansies, and especially violas, are the perfect companions for spring bulbs. After you plant the bulbs, plant pansies on top. They will flower both before and after the bulbs and the fading bulb foliage can be bent over and hidden beneath the pansy foliage. A favorite combination mixes yellow daffodils, which can be planted in the fall, with blue violas, or the pansy strain labeled Azure Blue, or one of the blues from the Crystal strain.

A less obvious place for pansies is about five or six feet in the air, in hanging baskets or in window boxes, simply because you can then enjoy them face-to-face. It would be tempting to make a window box just for pansies because they are so cute when viewed at eye-level. Seen up close, their faces resemble cats', with the streaks being the whiskers, and this is borne out in the name of one old-time pansy strain—Felix.

A mass planting of ranunculus shows the power of bulbs, especially if just one color is planted, though the few orange flowers in the field of yellow are a deft way of adding interest. These tender bulbs that are actually tubers shaped like a clump of bananas are planted in the fall in California, for joyful spring bloom.

A PLACE FOR BULBS

Bulbs are similar to annuals in that they are not permanent elements of the garden—at least not those parts that grow above ground. In California some bulbs must be replanted each year, while many others will apparently disappear for the summer. Those return the following fall or spring after spending part of the year underground where they must not be disturbed or overwatered.

Many daffodils, for example, will live from year to year, but not if the bulbs get too wet in summer. Therefore, you can't simply plant something else on top of daffodil bulbs, especially not other plants that need a lot of water. One solution is to plant something that needs little water—a low-growing herb or perennial, or a ground cover—at the time the bulbs are planted.

This gardening strategy also solves the problem of what to do with that withering foliage. After a bulb flowers the leaves must be left on until they naturally dry up (the plant needs time to move the food stored in its leaves to the bulb). If the bulbs are planted under something else, the browning bulb foliage can be tucked under the other plant's leaves.

Tied in Knots Another age-old way to deal with withered foliage is to tie it in a simple knot, which makes it appear that the gardener knows what he or she is doing, while it doesn't much improve the appearance of the garden bed. Yet another solution is to plant the bulbs behind other plants that are still growing so that as the bulbs wither, they are hidden by plants growing up in front of them. These are rather sophisticated ways of dealing with bulbs and require a good deal of gardening savvy, but a

garden notebook can help. Make a note of when the bulbs bloom and how long the foliage lasts.

Simpler Solutions Yet another way of dealing with the fading bulb foliage is to plant the bulbs off by themselves. A favorite spot for early spring bulbs is under a deciduous tree. There they get all the light they need in winter and early spring and protection from the sun in summer. Leaf litter provides an attractive mulch in summer and holds down weeds.

Or you can do what so many gardeners end up doing: Dig up the bulbs—after the foliage yellows—and store

them in a cool, dry place. You can even move them out of the garden before the foliage fades if you dig them up and temporarily plant them somewhere in the back, then store them away when the leaves are brown. The final solution is the simplest—just toss this year's bulbs out and buy new ones next year. In this case, be sure to dig up the bulbs right after flowering, while the stems are still strong enough to give you a handle for lifting the bulbs out of the ground. At the least, be sure to get the bulbs out while the foliage is still visible or you'll have the devil's own time finding them in the garden bed.

Plant Portrait

TRICKS WITH TULIPS

Before you decide that bulb planting will become an annual affair, be aware that it can be a lot of work. George de Gennaro, who is known for his beautiful food photography, plants some 15,000 bulbs each year and we asked him for this self-portrait at planting time so others could see just what is involved. Amazingly, he doesn't even look tired. Then he photographed this same spot in spring and you can see that it was worth all the effort.

Planting bulbs is no small task. Huge piles of earth are dug from the beds and piled to one side, after which wheelbarrows of sand and soil amendments are brought in. Compared to other garden chores, this is more like a military operation, but the result is spectacular. Twelve months later there are masses of bulbs blooming with dress parade precision at a regimented height—a spring so glorious that it is difficult to conceive of having such beauty in your own backyard.

What happens to these traditional Dutch bulbs is quite different in most Southern California gardens. Tulips, and especially hyacinths, tend to bloom at various heights and at different times, sometimes when they are barely out of the ground. Daffodils are less difficult to regiment, but we seldom see displays as picture-perfect as those in the de Gennaro garden.

The problem with tulip bulbs is their Dutch heritage. Bred in a bleak northern European climate, these bulbs do not expect January days with temperatures in the 80s. Though we cannot provide a mantle of snow, we can buffer them better against the occasional heat of a California winter and the strong sun of spring. Note the depth of the trench in the picture. Bulbs are not merely planted, they are buried. At least six inches of soil cover the bulbs, which means that the planting holes must be at least eight inches deep. The bulbs are safe from any hot winter weather beneath that blanket of soil—although it might be more apt to compare the insulating soil to a down quilt, since it is fluffy and light, more like potting soil than garden soil. Each year the de Gennaro bed is amended with organic matter while the sand cushioning the bed of bulbs gets mixed in each time the bed is prepared for planting. There is now a twenty-year accumulation of sand and organic soil amendments. The result is a soil so light and airy that it quickly drains away excess moisture and makes it easy for the bulbs to push their way upward to the surface.

The inch-thick layer of washed builders' sand added to the bottom of the planting hole is extra protection from a too-wet soil and helps hold the bulbs upright when the soil is shoveled back into the hole. Bulbs are spaced four to five inches apart atop this sand, with the exception of hyacinths, which are spaced five to six inches apart to allow room for their fat flower heads. Another clue for the sharp-eyed: Note when the bulbs are planted. This photo was taken on January 22, and some bulbs are already starting to sprout. De Gennaro plants late, very late, usually in January.

Before being planted, the tulip and hyacinth bulbs are refrigerated for a month or more in large coolers that are used by de Gennaro in the course of his food photography. It's a necessary step because these two bulb types need a simulated winter dormancy to bloom properly. Keep yours in the fridge.

This thirty-foot-long bed is only one of twelve such beds devoted to bulbs, all of them being in partial shade provided by flowering peach and nec-

tarine trees, dogwoods, birches, magnolias, and other deciduous trees that
are only partially leafed out when the
bulbs bloom. This slight shading
undoubtedly helps the tulips develop
the long stems they properly should
have, but often cannot achieve in
Southern California.

Anchoring the bulb beds are plantings of perennials such as coral bells
and columbine, and when the bulbs
are finished, more perennials are put
in. These later perennials include
masses of delphiniums, coreopsis, veronica, and marguerites; sometimes
summer annuals are added, to last
through the summer and fall. The
bushy marguerites are a particular
favorite as a summer filler since they
grow incredibly fast in the late spring.
Because these plants must be watered
in summer, all of the bulbs are taken
out after blooming; the tulips are
thrown away because they will not
flower a second year.

The timing of bulbs, perennials, and
annuals—when they should be planted
and when they bloom—works out surprisingly well. The permanent plantings of perennials—coral bells are the
favorite—are dug up and divided
when the bulb beds are prepared in
January. That works out neatly since
January is a good time for that chore
and perennials bloom better when
restarted in that fashion. January is
such a favorable time to divide the
practically dormant perennials that de
Gennaro is often able to leave huge
clumps of them sitting out of the
ground for days, with no ill effects,
while other work progresses.

The perennials planted after the
bulbs bloom are usually kept for only
one season, as though they were summer annuals. A good time to plant
perennials is when the bulbs finish in
May. De Gennaro plants most of his

from gallon cans, but our experience
indicates that even when planted from
four-inch pots in early May, perennials
will put on quite a show in June and
July, then carry a few flowers into fall.

May is also a good time to plant
summer annuals, and the bulb beds
usually can accommodate some zinnias
or impatiens as well. De Gennaro used
to plant chrysanthemums after the
bulbs were finished since the mums, in
turn, would be finished blooming in
the fall, before it was time to plant
bulbs again. But now de Gennaro

reserves the fall as a time to rest from
garden chores.

A permanent "planting" of rocks
also helps define the beds and somehow makes the bare earth of late fall
and midwinter (after the annuals and
some of the perennials have come out)
look quite natural while the garden
awaits bulbs. Once the bulbs are in, it
doesn't take long to see green shoots
begin to poke through the ground followed by buds and flowers—a benefit
of planting late.

In bloom at this point in the season

Planting bulbs can be big work, as you can see in the picture on page 110. Photographer George de Gennaro plants thousands each winter, digging huge trenches with an inch-thick layer of sand in the bottom to cradle the bulbs. The soil that goes back into the hole is thoroughly amended.

In spring, all the work pays off. On page 111 you see the same bed four months later, with 'Apricot Beauty' tulips in the foreground, mixed with Dutch iris and 'Soleil d'Or' narcissus. The deeper-colored tulips in the background are the variety 'Gudoshnik.'

(April) are the orange and red, 'Gudoshnik' tulips, a tulip named 'Apricot Beauty' the narcissus 'Soleil d'Or' mixed with a few Dutch irises and, in the path, a few crocuses planted with primroses. In this same bed, under a deciduous magnolia and several birches, are many other tulips and daffodils backed up by tall lilies, which bloom at different times.

Will this grand scheme work in a smaller garden? Absolutely. It will even work in containers; the big display of bulbs nearer the de Gennaro house is grown in containers. In a small garden, the principles of how deep to plant, when to plant, and how to prepare the soil still hold true. The only difference is the number of bulbs to plant. Just remember that a dramatic show of flowers depends on having a lot of one variety, so it's more effective to plant fewer kinds but more of them. Believe it or not, even the de Gennaros pass up different varieties of bulbs that they would like to try in favor of having a mass display. But as you can see, it works wonderfully.

Plant Portrait

MORE BULB STORIES

Bulbs needn't always be a lot of work. There are bulbs that can be planted in small holes and ways to use them that require fewer bulbs. Since bulbs are one of gardening's great mysteries, beginning as one thing—a pulpy mass in a papery husk—but developing into quite another, it seems only natural to describe their planting and flowering as if it were a mystery story recounted by a gumshoe gardener. Here are three intriguing cases to consider. They really happened this way.

A Classy Bulb October 25. Picking through a cardboard box at the nursery in Bay City, it looked too late for these bulbs. I could find only some that had sprouted and seemed ready to bloom. If they had been garlic or onions I would have left them there, but they were saffron, a classy bulb if there ever was one. I bought myself a dozen at forty-five cents.

October 26. I found the ideal spot for them, a narrow alley of soil between two concrete stepping stones. Under a hot October sun, I planted the bulbs just below the surface, with the sprouts above ground. I left no room between the bulbs, and in that skinny slit of soil they looked uncomfortable, like sardines in a can. They were a long way from their ancient Mediterranean home, but so are a lot of us in the City of Angels.

November 4. Nothing happened for eight days. A patient man would wait. I wasn't one. I dug up a bulb. It was making progress. In the last few days it had grown a dozen roots, each about three inches long. I carefully planted it again and went back to waiting.

November 11. It was one of those days that was already hot and dry and starting to fray the nerves—everything was too bright, the sky too blue. I stepped outside and through the glare of the early morning sun saw the saffron crocus in full flower. It was going to be a pretty day after all.

Around the Mediterranean, saffron is grown as a cash crop, like lima beans. I tried to imagine what a field full of saffron would look like. I couldn't. Even these few flowers were a spectacle. From the back door I could see the brilliant red saffron styles which yield that precious spice that sells for an arm and a leg and turns everything it touches a golden orange. Out in the garden, on hands and knees, I observed the light veining in the lilac petals that made the flowers look like feathers with the styles lying languidly across them, a fortune in saffron there for the picking. But I couldn't do it. Fortune would have to wait for another day.

November 12. Next morning the flowers were still there, and I found a lot of good reasons to walk by them during the day. But by night the show was over. Another round of flowers could be seen pushing their way through the dense bundle of leaves so there would be other days like this. Now it was time to harvest the styles. I picked them from between the wilted petals and set them aside to dry. Paella was their future and I made a note to plant more next year, though I managed to fill a tiny brown vial with this year's crop. Maybe I'd buy an acre down in Escondido. With saffron at eight dollars a bottle, I could see easy street right around the corner.

March 15. Months had passed since the last saffron flowers had faded, but I could still see them glowing in that too-bright October sun. Their leaves are just beginning to yellow now, and since they are long enough to trip over, I cut them back to about four inches so they would look like little tufts of grass. I

didn't want to trim them any further because they still needed to manufacture enough food to carry them through the long, hot Los Angeles summer. I look forward to their return—they're one of the few bulbs that come back every year.

Not a Weed October 21. They were the ugliest bulbs I had ever seen, dark and crusty like some rough loaf of bread you'd find on a monk's table. Labeled *Oxalis purpurea* Grand Duchess, they came in a plastic package filled with sawdust that the grower probably hoped would hide their ugliness. I bought some anyway. The picture on the package looked pretty, and they

were called Grand Duchess. I liked that. At home I gave them a hurried burial, covering them with just an inch of soil, spacing them about two inches apart, pointy part up. They lay between the stepping stones just outside the front door.

November 5. I had almost forgotten about those ugly little bulbs, but this morning there were a few clover-like leaves in that narrow space between the stepping stones. They were staying low as if they knew they could get stepped on.

November 11. Leaves are starting to fall from the trees, but the gap between the stepping stones is now a field of bright green shamrocks.

November 16. I got up late and went out into the bright morning, squinting, to fetch the paper. I never made it. There at my feet were dozens of tiny, white flowers glistening in the midday sun like miniature china set out for field mice. I went back in, poured a cup of coffee, and came out again to sit on the front steps. I could see why they were named Grand Duchess. This oxalis didn't look anything like the weedy variety that strangled parts of my garden. This one had elegant glove-white flowers.

January 1. The new year found the oxalis still in flower. They close up every night and only open when the sun is bright overhead, and if you spend too much time at the office you never see them. I make a point of not spending too much time at the office.

March 30. There are still a few flowers on the oxalis, but the foliage is beginning to yellow and collapse in the warming weather. This was one tough plant. It flowered for four-and-a-half months, got stepped on, and went without water at times. It might be a Grand Duchess, but no pansy.

Postscript. While the oxalis planted between the stepping stones has stayed and bloomed for three years, others planted in the best soil, in garden beds, have spread all over the place, becoming almost as weedy as the genuine oxalis. I now know to keep them confined and not to pamper them in the least.

Freesias Are Fragrant October 21. Freesias are pretty bulbs, long, slender, and covered with a fine mesh like a lady's stockings. It was hard not to buy a lot, but there was just one spot beside the path where, with a little shoehorning, I could fit some in. I bought a variety called Matterhorn. I had heard that the white varieties did best the second and third year and that they came close to being as permanent in the garden as any bulb. I filled a small, brown paper bag with them and brought them home.

November 25. I found the paper bag with the freesia bulbs under some seed catalogues on the workbench. What can I say? I had forgotten about them. But they didn't look any the worse for wear; I planted them, so close together that they were almost touching, and covered them with about two inches of soil. Now all I had to do was water and wait. In this bulb business there is a lot of waiting.

December 5. I didn't have to wait long. Slender green leaves are pushing

out of the ground so quickly you can hear them shove the soil aside.

March 6. The leaves have been up and ready for a long time and today the flowers make an appearance. They are not white like the 'Matterhorn Mountain', but creamy with a touch of yellow at their base. At night, in the still moist air, their fragrance is memorable, even from a distance recognizable as freesia. Like good perfume, it is neither overpowering nor too crisp.

March 30. Some flowers stand out in a crowd. Even though there are all sorts of flowers blooming at this time of year, the freesias hold their own. Flowers keep opening along their arching stems, like swans lifting off from a lake; the spent flowers can be pulled off to keep things tidy. I tidied up my few freesias, sat back on my haunches, and looked around to see where I could plant more next year. The garden looked swell.

From the ugly little oxalis bulbs in the top picture come the pretty white flowers and shamrock-like leaves shown below. The flowers are about 1½ inches across. This oxalis can spread just like the weedy kinds, so it is best to trap it between paving stones—the perfect place for this plant.

WHAT ABOUT WILDFLOWERS?

There are wildflowers and then there are "wildflowers." Genuine wildflowers are native to the area. Other flowers, native to other places, are often called "wildflowers" either because they grow so easily or because they are relatively "unimproved," that is, they haven't been turned into true garden flowers through hybridization or selection.

Pictured on these pages are examples of each and they illustrate two distinct ways to treat wildflowers. The spectacular field—what one expects—is full of "wildflowers." This is one of the seed fields of Environmental Seed Producers, the leading supplier of seed used in most wildflower mixes found at general nurseries. Though these mixes often contain California natives, such as the ubiquitous California poppy, they also contain many other flowers from all over the globe that have been found to grow with ease and have the simple look of a wildflower.

Real wildflowers—the genuine article—grow on a hillside overlooking the San Fernando Valley at the Theodore Payne Foundation in Sun Valley, California. The Foundation's purpose is to encourage the planting of California natives, and it is one of the primary suppliers of seed, most of it collected by volunteers from wild fields. This planting, put in by volunteer Kevin Connelly, grows with no supplemental irrigation. Rains germinate the seed and keep it going, so in some dry years the crop is a little meager. The planting was photographed during one of the drought years.

But even in a good year, it is a far cry from the other field of "wildflowers," and it is not what one usually imagines a field of wildflowers to look like. But climb to the top of this hill, and it looks right and smells right. You can step among the flowers as you can in the mountains or high desert. The colors are pure and bright—clear yellow, pure orange, bright blue—and the flowers are familiar to a day-hiker —California poppy, chia, tidy-tips, and thistle sage.

Growing Your Own Anyone who has grown *real* California wildflowers can tell you that growing these dainty wildlings, some of which are endangered in their natural areas, is somehow holier than other garden pursuits. There is no denying the impact of that waist-high field of "wildflowers" from a nursery mix. Which way to go?

Where you live, on what soil you garden, and on what scale you attempt to grow wildflowers should help you decide. If you live on flat land, with a clayey soil, most real California wildflowers will be difficult to grow. A better choice would be the mix "wildflowers," which undoubtedly will contain some true ones. Note that the "wildflowers" in the photograph are growing on prime agricultural land, with irrigation, a situation much more akin to the typical garden than the hilltop site at the Payne Foundation. Where wildflowers grew at one time, wildflowers will probably grow again. Here the soil and the site favor the natives.

Weeding Is the Chore You can probably grow either kind of wildflower in small garden beds, where it is not difficult to look after them. But if you expect to grow even a small meadowful, you should be prepared for a lot of work though you might be lucky and have the right combination of soil and location. And no weeds.

It is weeding that makes growing wildflowers such hard work. Though it might seem that nothing could be

There are wildflowers and then there are "wildflowers." The real thing is grown by Kevin Connelly on a hilltop at the Theodore Payne Foundation in Sun Valley, California. The other kind of "wildflowers" aren't necessarily native to the area (or even to the U.S.) but grow as if they were, with little help from man. Were they not so pretty, they might be called weeds. On page 117 a field of "wildflowers" is being grown for its seed. European red poppies and bachelor's buttons make a dazzling combination.

easier than growing flowers that ought to grow there naturally, once the soil has been disturbed, by gardening or by clearing, weeds quickly get the upper hand; they are successful invaders and have displaced many native plants. Even Kevin Connelly, who has planted many meadows of wildflowers, tackles only a small area at a time (as pictured here) when weeds are present or their seeds lie in wait.

Should you decide to give wildflowers a try, begin in the fall, before the rainy season arrives. First you

must clear the ground, being careful to disturb it as little as possible so you don't bury any weed seed (you'll see why). Then water thoroughly for several days to sprout the weed seed or bring persistent perennial weeds back to life. Once the weeds are up and growing (it takes several weeks), the easiest way to eliminate them is by spraying with a short-lived herbicide called Roundup or Kleenup. This will kill everything above ground and, since it's systemic, the roots as well, though a few perennial weeds might

survive even this. To be certain your land is entirely weed-free, water again after everything appears dead and wait to see if anything returns.

Time to Sow This should take you into December, the first month in which we can usually count on rains in Southern California. Now the wildflower seed can be sown and perhaps protected with bird netting so a few seeds remain to germinate. Rain or irrigation will bring up the wildflowers—also more weeds. As soon as you can tell one

from another, it's time to get down on hands and knees and begin separating the wheat from the tares.

There is no need to sow seed thickly, because, as Kevin Connelly puts it, "if one seed germinates, they all will." In fact, sowing thickly only makes weeding more difficult. Weeds that grow too close to a wildflower shouldn't be yanked out but should instead be cut off with small scissors. And don't think that all the weeds will have sprouted with the first rain; that's not their nature. To assure survival some seeds

germinate with each rain, in case others were routed by drought.

In defense of all this weeding, Kevin points out that people have to spend hours in the hot August sun weeding a dichondra lawn, but that with wild-flowers you can do your weeding in the cool of winter and spend August at the beach. Either way you go, with real wildflowers or their look-alikes, they can be the prettiest things you have ever planted. Just be prepared for some hard work if a meadowful is what you have in mind.

Garden Visit

A WILDFLOWER SUCCESS STORY

Perhaps the most unlikely place in the world to find wildflowers, or any native plant, is beside a spa. Think of it—drought-toughened California plants, valued because they need so little water, growing right next to it. For that matter, one does not expect to find a meadow of delicate wildflowers growing in the confines of an ordinary suburban backyard, but much about the garden pictured here is astonishing.

The big surprise is seeing the spa in the middle of a field of flowers. The next surprise is noting how well it blends into the overall picture. Except perhaps for the color of the water, it could be a puddle, or an isolated pool left behind at the end of the rainy season, for the spa has been worked into a natural-looking stream bed that runs diagonally across the garden. This was the inspired idea of the late Steven Dyer, with the actual design worked out and drafted by Richard Borkovetz. This man-made stream is no rushing cascade. Most of its length merely suggests water, since the only water is to be found in the spa. It is refreshingly subtle, content with being a simple, small stream bed, gone dry for the summer—marked only by its rocky bottom, a perfectly believable phenomenon.

The rocks that define the bed were all gathered in the Claremont area and are used most adroitly. They are all rather small, small enough to have been pushed down the mountainside by a stream this size, and there are not too many. The bed of the stream uses still smaller rock and loose gravel, and it doubles as a path across the garden, augmented near the patio's edge by a few concrete pavers. It follows the natural slope of the land and seeks the low ground as a stream naturally would. Its origins are hidden behind the garage and by shrubbery; its destination is also out of sight, in the side yard.

The plantings, including the wildflowers, are the work of Janet Dyer. Janet is a regular visitor to nearby Rancho Santa Ana Botanic Garden, the premier native plant garden in the state, and the influences of that magnificent public garden can be seen in this much smaller private one. Most of the plants are California natives, and all are drought-resistant because this garden gets by on natural rainfall with only a little supplemental irrigation in summer. There are other flowers from similar climates around the spa—the orange ice-plant and annual African daisy being the most conspicuous. But the flowers that make up the meadow are the genuine article—California poppy, bird's eyes gilia, blue thimble-flower, tidytips—wildflowers that could once very easily have grown on this gentle slope before it was reshaped into a tract of houses.

Originally, this area was a lawn, and after it was removed wildflower seed was sown and simply raked into the soil. Fall and winter rains brought the flowers up and nourished them. Surprisingly, nothing was done to the soil in preparation for planting, but Janet has been blessed with good fortune and an appropriate soil.

The soil is decomposed granite, a gritty, loose soil that drains excess water quickly. Each summer after the wildflowers finish up, Janet waits for them to scatter their seed, then cuts them to the ground, leaving the litter where it lies. In summer the ground is left dry and the shrubs and succulents in the garden carry the show, but with the first rains of autumn, up come the colorful wildflowers, all on their own.

Resembling a quiet pool in an otherwise dry Southwest streambed, a spa is surrounded by wildflowers. California poppies are the light orange brushstrokes (the deep orange are the flowers of an ice plant) and they are easy to grow. More trying are the dainty lavender bird's eyes gilia in the background and the yellow tidytips. The rocks and gravel that make up the dry streambed are also used for a diagonal path across the garden so the wildflowers don't get stepped on.

CHAPTER
5
COLOR,
HARMONY, AND
CONTRAST

Sometimes a simple scheme is the best color scheme of all, especially for a beginning gardener on the first few tries. The cream flowers of a Pacific Coast iris named 'Chimes' harmonize nicely with an old white picket fence in the picture on pages 120–121.

Pink flowers and gray foliage are a classic and very simple color scheme. The pink is a spreading and somewhat rambunctious Mexican evening primrose. The gray foliage belongs to an artemisia.

SIMPLE SCHEMES

Have you ever picked a flower and carried it, like a paint chip, to another plant to see if the colors go together? One would not dare to paint a room and put curtains, rugs, and sofas in it without carefully evaluating the compatibility of their colors, yet in the garden color schemes seldom get such consideration. Perhaps this is because flowers are pretty no matter what their color, or perhaps because the colors of flowers are so much more complex than the colors on a fabric or a paint chip; on the one hand we are delighted with flowers, but at the same time we are not too sure why. Sometimes we are not even sure what color they are. Some flower colors are particularly tricky. What is a "blue" flower, for instance? Few are truly blue.

Observation gives us something concrete to work with. If we take a thoughtful second look we might note what colors we like and which ones harmonize or go together. And perhaps we might make special note of those that do not. What we like is no small part of this decision-making process because different people have very different likes and dislikes and most find that their ideas change as they develop as gardeners.

Change Colors change too. Another reason to keep your own garden notes is that colors look very different in different parts of the world and under different skies. California, for instance, has intense contrast of light and dark, the shadows being so much blacker, the sunny spots, so much more glaring. It is almost impossible to look at both at the same time. The eye just can't handle the difference, and the camera cannot accommodate it, which is why so many gardens are photo-graphed on overcast days.

Under England's often cloudy skies, the light is much softer and the contrast between shady and open areas hardly noticeable. In Southern California, coastal gardeners also live with overcast skies almost every day, while inland gardeners hardly ever see a cloud. These two situations call for a very different selection of colors. Color changes with the time of day as well as with the seasons, hues appearing warmer and darker when the sun is rising or setting, brighter in summer, and cooler in winter.

Impossible? If the question of color in the garden sounds impossibly complicated, especially for men, who have much less experience with color than women do, there are simple ways to approach it. Even if you have only learned that a red tie looks good with a blue blazer, you can be on your way because it's possible to create very simple color schemes in the garden, which can then develop with your knowledge and ability into something far more complex and challenging.

Finding satisfying color schemes can become a gardener's lifework, along with learning how to grow the particular plants one needs to create these schemes. In modern times, in our smaller gardens, this often becomes the main point of garden planning. Once those paths are in, the background planted, and the beds for flowers in place, we could sit back and happily watch things grow—if it weren't for the fact that we will probably never get the colors quite right. We might not even recognize the possibilities at first. Most of us are thrilled when a bed of mixed flowers first comes into bloom, but after a year or two of growing them, we begin to see that there is work to be done.

Hot colors are sometimes hard to use in a garden, but one solution is to put them all together. Deep red dianthus, hot red penstemon, and bright red roses grow in colorful harmony with the blue-gray foliage of a grass named Festuca ovina glauca *and the "blue" of lobelia.*

HOT, COOL, AND TRUE BLUE

Gardeners have discovered that you can divide nearly all flowers into two groups—those that are colored red through blue, and those that are yellow through orange. If at first you only plant flowers from one or the other group, you will have simplified things greatly without limiting yourself, because the colors within each group are most likely going to harmonize.

The red-through-blue group is particularly easy and pleasing because, even though red is a member, these colors are cool and comfortable to look at. They look best in cool light, under overcast skies in winter or early spring. There is one condition—the red must be pure red, without a hint of orange, perhaps just a hint of blue.

An orange cast makes red hot and moves it into the other group. Be particularly careful with roses, since the red of roses can go either way, toward orange or toward pink. Pink is probably the most common color in the red-through-blue group, and it is a very easy color to live with in the garden. There are hundreds of pink flowers, and you can even have flowers that shade toward salmon without upsetting the color cart.

Blue? True blue flowers are practically nonexistent, though hundreds are called that. Agapanthus, campanulas, pansies, salvias, veronicas, and a hundred other plants are called "blue," but in reality they are violet or purple. While violet or purple flowers harmonize with pink and true red, they contrast with yellow, in a striking way. The so-called blue-bedder salvia, for instance, blends nicely with pink flowers, but it makes yellow flowers seem absolutely dazzling.

Yellow and Orange Yellow and orange are much hotter colors, and consequently such flowers are harder to handle. But they are invaluable in summer when paler, more pastel colors almost disappear in the brilliant sunlight. Bright yellows and oranges do not mix easily with other colors, so they are often used alone; the exceptions are the most subtle shades, which will blend with other flowers if they are kept in the minority. However, yellow and orange flowers can make an exciting accent in a red-blue scheme. With time and some experimenting you can discover how to use both groups of colors in the same bed, remembering that one group should always be decidedly dominant.

The Simplest Scheme Using only one color is the simplest scheme of all, and yellow is the first color to come to mind because so many flowers are yellow, or what gardeners call "gold." For instance, use tall golden gloriosa daisies for a background, with tall American or African marigolds in front of them. In front of these can go the shorter, smaller-flowered French marigolds, and in front of them the short golden fleece *(Dyssodia).* Don't worry if they are lemon yellow, orange, or somewhere in between—they all are variations of yellow and will blend beautifully.

WHITE, GRAY, AND GREEN

It has been said that white is the peacemaker in the garden. Wherever one suspects that two colors might not go together, separate them with white flowers and harmony will be restored. White flowers have the gift of bringing a delightful airiness with them and keeping a garden from seeming congested. They seem to glow in the distance, and at dusk they have a

certain magic when other colors all but disappear. Like shafts of sunlight, they add luminosity to the plantings.

In a garden using flowers of only a single hot color try adding white flowers to cool things down. Leave a few open spots in the front row for the low-growing *Chrysanthemum paludosum,* which looks like a miniature Shasta daisy, and back between the marigolds plant the real Shasta daisy and maybe a few plants of feverfew. All of these have white flowers and they will bring a little peace to this hot composition.

A crafty gardener always has a few white-flowered plants standing by at planting time.

Gray Foliage Gray or silvery leaves act much like white flowers. They too can mediate differences between other colors, but they are especially valuable when more light is wanted in the garden because they reflect it so well. Planted in a garden bed that is becoming too green and dark, they add airiness and open up the composition.

Gray-leaved plants make a garden appear sunnier simply because we associate gray-leaved plants with sunny climates, which is where most of them originate. Because gray-foliaged plants reflect light, they are best put off in the distance, though the temptation is to use them up close because their foliage is so interesting. But they attract the eye when they are at a remove, becoming a misty gray, and seeming to make the garden much deeper than it really is.

Green Flowers With so much green foliage in the garden, green flowers might seem to be redundant. But they act like white flowers and help separate conflicting colors in the garden, adding openness. Green flowers have a certain

fascination and are a fine conversation piece. There are not many kinds, but one is especially useful and easy to find, if only in seed catalogs. It is the pale green-flowered form of the common bedding nicotiana, a native American plant that blooms for months with a nice growth to boot.

Getting Started Though entire books could be devoted to color in the garden—or to the subject of color alone—there is nothing quite like plunging in and finding out what works. Pick a garden bed and decide on the basic scheme, be it the red-pink-blue colors, or the yellows and

oranges. Begin collecting plants with these colors and then try sketching a color plan. Draw blobs of color and see how one looks next to the other. There is no need to get the colors absolutely right. Try contrasting dark and light shades of the same color for emphasis. The dark shades often look like shadows of the lighter colors, and this contrast gives depth to the planting. Now add white, gray, and green wherever airiness is needed, or peacemaking between two colors.

A surprisingly sophisticated flower garden can be constructed in this fashion, with surprisingly little expertise.

White flowers and gray foliage act like shafts of light in the garden, and they can also work as peacemakers, settling disputes between other warring colors. On page 126, three of the best perennials with gray foliage are lamb's ears, snow-in-summer, and dusty miller. Blue star creeper is the ground cover between the stepping stones in this garden designed by Robert Fletcher.

Coral bells, on page 127, is one of the best of the white flowers and will grow in some shade. This is the native California species, Heuchera maxima.

Plant Portrait

A PORTFOLIO OF WHITE FLOWERS

Warm summer evenings are the best time to appreciate the magical appeal of white flowers. Their cool presence lingers long after the sun has set, their pale petals glowing in the twilight. Many perfume the air with sweet summery fragrances; in the garden, scent is somehow associated with the color white. The vining jasmine and stephanotis, common gardenia and citrus blossoms, and the not-so-common white heliotrope are some of the sultriest.

Many white flowers need no introduction, but there are others deserving of more recognition. The white heliotrope, for instance. It is uncommon at nurseries and actually began as an indoor plant offered by Logee's Greenhouses in Danielson, Connecticut. In much of the country it can be grown outdoors as an annual because it develops so quickly, but in California it becomes a long-lasting vining shrub, thriving in partial shade or full sun. It is very easy to grow, rambling at first among its neighbors until it mounds up to become a small haystack of a shrub about four feet tall and eight feet across. Or it can be trained to climb a trellis. It has a delicious, sort of candy-store scent.

Two more summer bloomers are the white *Scabiosa caucasica*, with flowers growing atop twenty-four-inch stems while the foliage occupies but a square foot of ground, and the white yarrow—*Achillea millefolium*—also a fine flower for cutting and about the same height. *Achillea millefolium*, which lives up to the thousand leaves in its Latin name, spreads on underground roots to make quite a patch. It shouldn't be planted where it might overwhelm lesser plants.

The tall spires in the garden pictured here belong to *Verbascum chaixii*,

Two examples of white flowers for the garden are shown on page 128. Top, the popular double Shasta daisy named 'Esther Read,' and below, the rare but rambunctious white heliotrope.

Designer Christine Rosmini planted one whole section of her garden white. The tall spires belong to the rare Verbascum chaixii; *each has a royal purple center. At their base is a white scabiosa, and just behind it is a white lantana. In the background are white 'Iceberg' roses and yarrow.*

one of my favorite plants, a garden gem waiting to be discovered by more plant prospectors. It develops a two-foot-wide clump of large green leaves and sends up spire after spire of glistening white flowers, each with a dazzling royal purple center that can only be discerned on close inspection. It is a perennial arising from big carrot-like roots and its tall white shafts add

drama to the flower bed or border.

White flowers are so cool and pleasing that they can become a gardener's addiction, leading to all-white schemes such as the one pictured here in a Los Angeles garden. Inspired by the all-white garden of Victoria Sackville-West at Sissinghurst Castle in Kent, designer Chris Rosmini set aside one corner of her garden exclusively for

white flowers. All of the flowers mentioned in this chapter are in it, plus white lantana that surrounds the verbascum, and white delphiniums that tower in the background. The best white rose for landscaping is 'Iceberg,' used by many designers as peacemaker and anchor in garden beds. Other white or near-white roses are 'Honor,' 'Pristine,' and 'Sweet Afton.'

Plant Portrait

A PORTFOLIO OF GRAY FOLIAGE

Most gray-leaved plants developed in sun-drenched climates, where they adopted this coloration as a defense; the tiny white hairs that cover the leaves, or the white, waxy coating—glaucousness—reflect the heat and trap a tiny bit of cooling moisture near the leaf's surface.

Gray-leaved plants may be bluish, greenish, or silvery; in the garden each shade can be used to a particular advantage. Silvery plants are the boldest. They stand out among the other flowers, as if illuminated by their own personal shaft of sunlight. Blue-gray plants are the coolest looking and are best mixed with green plants that have a hint of blue in their leaves, or with lavender and purple flowers. Gray-green plants are the most common and offer an image of softness and subtlety when mixed with other plant-

ings. Gray-green plants are especially attractive mixed with pink flowers.

Purple, pink, and white are the colors traditionally thought to go best with gray-leaved plants, but the possibilities go beyond the traditional. The brilliant cherry red of a rose named 'Double Delight' is close to perfection when planted near the gray foliage of lamb's-ears. Soft yellows that are not too golden are also delightful near gray foliage and, in fact, many gray-leaved plants do have yellow flowers.

Lamb's ears and lychnis are two of the prettiest and most useful gray-greens. Lamb's-ears (*Stachys byzantina,* formerly *S. lanata)* is aptly named; the leaves are soft and silky—one is almost tempted to say cute and cuddly. It is probably the most useful of the gray-leaved plants—a favorite of the English gardener Gertrude Jekyll, who knew so well how to use plants in the garden. At the front of a flower

Gray color schemes at work: A ground covering of blue fescue in front of the taller dusty miller on page 130, photographed in the parking lot of the Huntington Botanical Garden.

Landscape architect Isabelle Greene used shades of gray foliage to carry the eye far into the distance. The silver of Senecio leucostachys *in the foreground gives way to the steely gray of St. Catherine's lace, then to the gray green of English lavender's foliage and the gray carpeting of yellow-flowered gazanias.*

border it is unsurpassed; in England we find it a traditional choice for planting in front of roses, and a good many rose plantings in America would be immensely improved placed behind a row of lamb's ears to hide their bare bases. The plant is equally effective bordering a concrete walk or drive, where its gray leaves are so harmonious with the color of the concrete that they lend elegance to this otherwise drab material.

A perennial, lamb's ears spreads rapidly in good soil and warm weather to become a six-inch-tall mat measuring several feet across and dense enough to discourage weeds. Should it spread too far, you can cut it back; it is not invasive and is easy to pull out. In winter, older leaves shrivel, but enough remain to keep the planting presentable. It flowers in spring with small pink blossoms too modest to be noteworthy. Old clumps eventually deteriorate, but it is easy to start a new planting from pieces that have rooted.

Lychnis coronaria 'Alba' is a white-flowered form of the common perennial magenta-flowered Maltese cross. Its flowers, which occur only occasionally, are graceful and airy, but the dense crisp clump of leaves is unusually handsome—each leaf a shimmering gray-green edged with silver hairs. The plant grows slowly to make a six-inch-tall clump about eighteen to twenty-four inches across.

An example of the blue-gray coloration is blue fescue *(Festuca ovina glauca)*. Most often seen as a ground cover in California, it is even more effective used more sparingly, planted here and there in natural-looking clumps—small ten-inch-tall tufts of grass among the flowers—in meadow-like fashion. *Festuca* 'Bronzeglanz' is an even wispier gray-green grass. Silvery-gray plants are the most

striking because of the way they reflect the light. One of the prettiest is a yarrow *(Achillea)* named 'Moonshine'. The ferny leaves make a low, handsome clump that slowly spreads until it measures several feet across. This yarrow does not seem weedy as so many

do. The distinctive flat-topped flower spikes, a clear, clean lemon-yellow color, grow about eighteen inches tall. Planted in front of blue agapanthus, they offer a fine spectacle. The foliage has a soothing fragrance.

Perhaps the most silvery plant is the

A dianthus named 'Jealousy,' on page 132, not only has gray foliage but white flowers. A small green eye in the center of each flower inspired the flower's intriguing name.

Lamb's ears, on page 133, is the perfect plant for the foreground with soft, velvety-gray foliage and a low, tidy habit of growth, at least for the first year. It is a traditional choice for planting in front of roses, as it hides the bare base of the bush and harmonizes with the rose's reddish foliage.

common dusty miller *(Senecio cineraria)*, a shrubby perennial with leaves that are nearly white. Often sold as a bedding plant, it will grow to about two feet around, eventually needing a bit of pruning (or replacing) to stay neat. The flowers are most often cut off before they bloom because, being a rather plain yellow, they aren't harmonious with the rest of the plant. But if there is a place in the garden where you want foliage to pop right out of its surroundings, the senecios can't be beat.

Plant Portrait

A PORTFOLIO OF GREEN FLOWERS

Avid gardeners sometimes find themselves heading down some curious avenues. Take, for example, plants with green flowers. Grass is green; flowers are supposed to be colorful. However, once you've discovered green flowers, they become plants that you simply must have. Beyond their surprising coloration, green flowers are similar to white flowers in that they can be planted anywhere in the garden without causing a ruckus; they won't compete with other colors and they soften harsh contrasts.

Corsican hellebore *(Helleborus lividus corsicus)* is an unusually bold and handsome plant. It grows as clumps of stems in true perennial fashion, usually attaining a height of two feet and growing to several feet across after a few years. The apple-green flowers begin to appear in late fall and, in California, last well into summer. What makes this hellebore so useful is its ability, once it becomes established, to survive in shade with merely a spattering of sunlight and with little care. It will even compete successfully with tree roots or grow on the north side of a house.

Several euphorbias have greenish flowers, but *Euphorbia wulfenii* has shocking shamrock-green flowers that begin in January and last into June. It grows as a slowly spreading clump of three-foot-tall stems. As with many euphorbias, this one can tolerate less than ideal irrigation and some shade, though the flowers are greener in good light. For a yearly restart, cut the entire clump to the ground in the early fall.

'Green Goddess' is an absolutely elegant calla lily that is treated somewhat like a weed at the Huntington Botanical Gardens in San Marino,

and a fad at florists. It is tough and tall, growing to a height of four or five feet. Flowers begin in February and keep blooming through spring. It will grow in sun or shade and is, therefore, another candidate for the difficult north side of a house. It gets along with infrequent watering but thrives with lots.

The chartreuse-flowered form of the common shrimp plant *(Justicia brandegeana,* formerly *Beloperone guttata)* makes a showy four-foot-tall shrub that seems forever in flower. It prefers partial shade where its color becomes less yellow, although if there is not enough light the growth might be a bit lax. An eastern exposure is ideal. It likes water but can get by with little.

CHAPTER
6
DETAILS
MAKE THE
DIFFERENCE

An old cart filled with impatiens, bedding begonias, ivy, and grape ivy is the finishing touch for the shady corner of a patio, seen on pages 136–137.

Other finishing touches are much smaller—a few rocks and pebbles at the base of a container, and some very small plants to its right can do the trick. The little fern is the tough sun-loving Cheilanthes fendleri, *normally found in rock gardens; the pink flowers belong to a true geranium.*

THOSE LITTLE PLACES

Pebbles, pools of water, plants tucked here and there and similar elements are the finishing touches for a garden—the embroideries, the details you see on second look that keep you fascinated. Adding these embellishments is relatively easy, but the idea often does not occur to gardeners until they have gardened for a great many years. That's perhaps just as well, because these little touches cannot be planned in advance. The spots where they work best—the small places in the garden—do not exist until the basic bones of the garden are established and have perhaps fleshed out and grown a bit.

Plants—smaller than those found in the flower bed—are the most fascinating details because no matter how often you visit the garden, they will always look different, changing day by day, or even hourly, and certainly with the seasons and the years.

Little Plants Small bulbs are an excellent example. The crocus pictured in this chapter, a rare species named *Crocus goulimyi*, only discovered in 1955 growing wild in southern Greece, has its own little place beside a path in my garden. Anywhere else it might be overwhelmed, but here, protected on one side by the path and on another by a large rock and a very dwarf eugenia, it holds its own. It flowers in the fall when this particular spot happens to be bathed in the low sunlight of the autumn months. It is the perfect place for this plant, but I could not have planned for it, even though I was on the lookout. In good time, as the garden evolved, the spot simply appeared. I also made sure that such little places would occur by not filling the garden chock-full at first, and by

making paths and flower beds somewhat irregular in shape so there would be nooks and crannies in which to tuck treasures.

Little plants such as this *Crocus goulimyi* often turn out to be the most delightful in the garden; I always look forward to the month of October when this crocus is in bloom. When finished, it is a trifle untidy for the entire winter; in summer, it is completely dormant, so its season is just one short month. But when it is not flowering it does not leave a gaping sore in the side of the garden since it occupies such a small space.

Many plants make equally suitable details, or finishing touches, for a garden. A number of plants sold as ground covers (such as ajuga) actually work better planted in little places, and many plants sold as alpine or rock garden treasures are perfect candidates for the nooks and crannies in the garden.

And Pebbles Mulches of pebbles, such as those surrounding crocus bulbs, are another kind of finishing touch, though their contribution is not so much to add interest as to neatly hem the garden—where the rough edges show, where the soil is too obvious, or where little plants need a setting and some protection from hard rain. They also add another texture, one halfway between the smooth, hard surface of paving and the soft, rumpled velvet of plants.

ACCESSORIES FOR THE GARDEN

While little plants and pebbles could be considered finishing touches, other details in the garden might be compared to the furnishings and accessories in a room. Boulders, rocks, pebbles, and stones are the most natural accessories. Used with restraint, they become solid anchors for the garden and foils for special plants, but there is a danger of overdoing their presence, especially in areas where rocks are not found naturally.

A Place for Boulders, Rocks, Stones, and Pebbles For a rock to look at home in the garden there must be some logic in its placement. Large rocks, for instance, are best buried with only a third of their bulk showing, rather like an iceberg at sea. This is an old rule of landscaping but one hard to follow if you have just spent money commensurate to its size for a large rock or have expended energy lugging it into the back yard. Refined rocks, like refined people, do not display everything they've got.

In nature, rocks are seldom found just lying about at random, unless they are at the base of a hill or in a gully where water or gravity may have carried them. Used as if they were in a dry stream bed, you can leave most of the rock exposed above ground, but other smaller stones should also be evident. The best way to see how rocks should be used in the garden is to imitate nature: large boulders are usually buried up to their necks; smaller rocks are always in the company of stones and pebbles and are usually gradated by the stream that deposited them, not randomly mixed.

Or you might use rocks like sculpture, selecting a particularly interesting specimen and displaying it in a special place.

Sculpture Plants that are either naturally sculptural or are made so, such as topiary—plants trimmed to a shape they would not have in nature, perhaps a pyramid or a rabbit—are accessories for the garden, not unlike a small sculpture set on the mantle. Sculpture

itself can be used as a detail, though it is difficult to keep a piece of sculpture from stealing the show and becoming a focal point of the garden. Plants growing in containers are somewhat sculptural and extremely versatile as garden accessories because they can be moved around until just the right place is found for them.

Birds and butterflies—the real thing, that is—could even be considered finishing touches, and you can add plants such as butterfly weed to the garden that will attract these lively and colorful visitors.

Furniture Outdoor furniture is certainly another finishing touch, one that should be considered early on but only in the sense that you must leave enough room and a suitable place for it. What furniture will look best and, for that matter, which way it will face, is best decided after the structure of the garden is built. Besides a location for the obvious table and chairs, you will want to keep an eye open for places where a bench might be welcome, though your feet and legs may suggest this location before your eyes do. Where would you like to sit down and rest, and what view might you like to contemplate while catching your breath between garden chores?

No one place in the garden is perfect so a variety of seating choices is called for. Put seating where it is bathed in morning sun, a bench that is in shade in the middle of the day, and maybe one that is lit at night. Is one flower bed especially pretty when back-lit by the sun? Then put a place to sit in front of it. There is really no way to plan for this, and these places must be discovered after the garden is in. Don't overlook frivolous furnishings such as a swing hanging from the largest tree in the yard. Imagine how wonderful that would be to come upon unexpectedly.

On Second Look These details are what you see on second look and shouldn't detract from the overall picture of the garden, which means they must be used with subtlety and be scaled appropriately. The garden's path should still command the situation, and the focal point should not have strong competition. The background should carry the most weight and the flower beds be the prettiest elements. But once these things are taken care of, it's time to add the details, one by one, as they occur to you, and as spots for them open up.

Garden Visit

A COMPACT CITY GARDEN WITH BRILLIANT TOUCHES

This little garden depends heavily on small details. There is more to look at, more to discover here than in most large gardens. Every square inch has been thought out and carefully planted or ornamented in such a way that no matter where you look you will see something of interest. Los Angeles landscape designer Chris Rosmini used even the walls that shield the garden from the busy street as places to plant. Succulents grow in little balconies and make a living mural that is the unquestioned focal point for the garden.

Most of the paving blocks are spaced far enough apart for plants to grow between them, and where plants might get stepped on, shiny little pebbles take their place. Very tiny plants grow in tall flue-tile planters where they are safe from all the dangers that beset small flora—feet, competition from other plants, and flooding—everything except snails. Most of these minuscule plants are gem-like alpines ordered from rock-garden specialty nurseries, and they need the best of drainage.

Other details, while not miniature, are smaller than they usually are: a fountain, for example, contained within a large concrete pot, or outdoor lights that make the garden useful at night. But more than any other elements, plants are used as the details in this garden—a great variety of leaf and flower colors, shapes, and textures, delightful every time they are rediscovered. There is even a small sculpture sitting inside the fountain, a secondary focal point after the first overwhelming sight of the wall of succulents. The sound of the fountain is also a detail of sorts.

On the other side of the fence on this page is a street; the wall of succulents hides the view while a small fountain masks the noise.

Sedums and other succulents grow in the wall's planting pockets. Water runs from one pocket to the next through drainage slits.

Pre-colored concrete flue tiles provide homes for rock-garden plants that might otherwise be lost or trampled underfoot. The gray mat and almost white leaves belong to two species of the Raoulia.

Plant Portrait

PLANTS BETWEEN PAVING STONES

One of the first things visitors notice about my garden is that I grow plants within the paths. They can scarcely fail to notice since one could literally trip over the plants, though nobody has yet. My paths are made of pavers roughly two-by-two feet in size. These are set on a two-inch-deep base of tamped sand with approximately a two-inch space between pavers, and this gap is wide enough to plant in.

The plants are a welcome respite from all that paving, which, while it may be practical, is still a lot of hard surface. The plants that overgrow it help diminish the size of the path without lessening its usefulness. They also help blend the edges of the garden where it meets the path, contributing to a more natural look. The flower beds don't end abruptly, nor does the lawn, but one bleeds into the other.

The spaces between and around stepping-stones make perfect homes for many small plants including the summer bulb Zephyranthes grandiflora *on page 142 and the tiny woolly yarrow,* Achillea tomentosa, *page 143. The purple flowers belong to the wandering* Verbena rigida.

organic matter, put it back in, and plant. Then I put a mulch of small rock around the plants which also keeps feet from getting stuck in the gap. The path gets watered with the flower beds.

"Don't the plants get stepped on?" On occasion, but they are actually quite visible, framed as they are in concrete. In fact, this is where I grow some of my choicer plants, little rock-garden-sized plants and bulbs. Even the kids have learned to maneuver around them with their bikes and various other vehicles, and newcomers to the garden tend to tread lightly at first, as if they were stepping over a rattler sunning himself in the middle of the path. In effect, it works much like the zigs and zags in Japanese paths, slowing one down so there is time to observe the garden and soak up whatever is there. But when you need to get a wheelbarrow down the path, you just roll right over them. They bounce back. Plants that spread too far into the center of the path do get stepped on and learn to grow lower, to hide down in the cracks.

I have found these plants to be the toughest: a little Australian violet *(Viola hederacea)* that grows in shady sections; a tough gazania-like plant named *Drymondia* that could probably be run over by a tank; a low-growing yarrow and dianthus that would be overwhelmed by other plants if they were grown anywhere else in the garden; creeping oregano and thyme that smell good when they get stepped on; and the creeping, but fairly tall (for a path), *Verbena rigida* that brings a most casual air to the planting when it is in full flower.

This informality is perhaps what I like most about planting in paths—it's short of looking weedy, but does look overgrown, suggesting that the gardener is not too stern a fellow.

Planting in the middle of pathways is not an original idea. Vegetation springs up on its own quite naturally wherever there is a crack to grow in, and other gardeners before me have taken advantage of the little planting spaces, but plants in a path still surprise this most practical modern generation.

"Don't people trip on them?" No, because they are not in the center of the path but off to either side. "Well, what about weeds?" There is no short-age of these, to be sure, but I have modified a little weeder that fits between the pavers and makes short work of unwanted plants. It is called a "Cape Cod Weeder" and came from tool supplier Walt Nicke in Topsfield, Massachusetts. I filed off about an inch of the blade so it is precisely the width of the gap between the pavers.

"How do you plant in those narrow gaps?" I use a narrow trowel. I dig up the soil, amend it with sand and

Pots can be artful or amusing, like the one on page 144. The author built one large trough in the shape of a pig (the inspiration came from an early American weather vane) and filled it with herbs and flowers. The lattice ends hide the boards that make the actual planter box. A piece of rope serves as the tail.

A study in proportion on page 145, these pots hold sweet peas, a surprising candidate for container culture. The sweet peas climb natural bamboo poles.

A PLACE FOR POTS

Plants growing in containers are perhaps the best accessory of all because they can be changed and moved about with ease, and can be put in places where flowers might not otherwise be able to grow—on the steps leading to the back door, for instance, or against a blank wall beneath a window, and beside a driveway where there is no room for anything else.

Plants grown in containers can be dramatically sculptural—a spiny yucca, for example—or flamboyantly colorful—a potful of zinnias or the piñata-colored portulaca. They become minor focal points or strong secondary accents of interest. At the very least, a plant in a container may simply be pleasant or utilitarian—a pot of herbs for example—and helps flesh out the garden composition, adding soft color or greenery.

Band-Aids I often use potted plants as Band-Aids, to hide a scar in the garden. If something poops out before it should, or perhaps grows too tall and leggy, a potted plant on the path or

patio in front of the offending plant covers up the eyesore, just like a Band-Aid.

Potted plants can also distract the eye from parts of the garden that are not at their finest. They can even be the primary focal point, especially if you do what large public gardens often do—keep pots of colorful flowers growing in back somewhere so they can be moved out front as the contents of other pots have finished blooming.

Collectibles Many collectible plants, such as orchids and bromeliads, or rare ferns and begonias, are best kept in containers. First, because their special needs can be looked after (primarily the need for a special kind of soil), but also because they are so unusual that they do not fit visually with the rest of the garden, and a container sets them apart.

Relatively cold-tolerant orchids, bromeliads, and staghorn ferns are particularly useful in Southern California since the plants can be mounted directly to slabs of wood or cork and hung on vertical surfaces, such as walls and fences, where nothing else could grow. They are epiphytic plants that, in the tropics, naturally grow up from the ground and attach themselves to trees. The kinds needing some soil can be grown in small pots with special hangers that allow them to be grown on vertical surfaces. Should it get too cold, they can be taken down and temporarily moved to a warmer spot, even indoors, for the night.

Another Art Growing plants in containers is quite a different gardening technique than growing them in the ground. A potted plant would not last a week without care; it is entirely dependent upon the gardener for water and nutrients. Watering at all times is essential, but during the summer, plants in containers may need to be watered every day. Since they require regular care—even when you are on vacation—it is important that when you first plan your garden, you make sure your pots and containers can be watered easily and quickly. You should be able to reach them with a hose without knocking down other plants in the process. It's a good idea to keep a collection of watering cans scattered throughout the garden, filled at all times. If they are handsome ones, the cans become a sort of garden ornament.

The Same Rules Apply When arranging planted containers in the garden, apply the same principles you use when planning your flower beds. Flowers in containers also look elegant as formal compositions (as on the steps pictured here) or grouped in casual clusters of three's and five's. Small pots set behind large pots give the illusion of being further away, so if you put large containers in the foreground with small ones further back, you stretch the apparent length of the garden.

Garden Visit

PARADISE AT PARKLABREA

At Parklabrea, the large apartment complex in the heart of downtown Los Angeles, 1,150 small concrete patios are set among the communal courtyards of the aging development. One of these seven-by-seventeen-foot slabs is as flower-filled as an English country garden. Not surprisingly, it is tended by English gardeners who cannot understand why every patio is not as pretty as theirs.

Film producer and writer Ronnie Kinnock and his wife, Beryl, brought their love of flowers—and the knack for growing them successfully—with them from their London townhouse. Confronted by the concrete, it was obvious to them that ordinary flower pots simply wouldn't do. So the Kinnocks devised the clever containers seen here. The wooden troughs are raised above the height of the windowsills, on trestle-like legs, thus they can be appreciated from inside the apartment as well as from the patio. Elevated like this, they add a third dimension of height to the otherwise flat patio. The gardener doesn't have to stoop while working among the containers that have still another advantage and asset for renters—they are portable. A few planters are double-deckers not unlike London's famous buses: plants that enjoy the sun ride on top, shade plants below.

What grows in the containers? The Kinnocks' favorite is lobelia, "as close to gentian blue" as they could find in California. They grow the Crystal Palace strain, which blooms most of the year. Other favorites include phlox, sweet alyssum, ivy geranium, and a little white daisy named *Chrysanthemum paludosum*—all proper residents of a country garden, but thriving here in the middle of a large city.

Masses of purple lobelia, white sweet alyssum, and red geraniums spill from homemade containers that conceal the stark concrete patio of an inner-city apartment complex in Los Angeles. Some of the wooden containers are double-deckers with room downstairs for plants that can tolerate a little shade.

WATER IN THE GARDEN

Nothing brings sparkle to a garden like a bit of water. It needn't be torrents, or cascades, or even a small lake or pool. It can be as modest as a bird bath, but in the right location water will be a cool and refreshing sight in hot weather, the play of light from its surface bringing delight on all but the gloomiest of days. Even on a rainy day, water adds another element and another level of complexity to the design of a garden.

When you add a recirculating pump, water even sounds refreshing, though care must be taken because a steady splash can also become as annoying as the drip of a faucet. It takes some experimenting to find just the right combination of factors that makes splashing water sound good. The play of water must be tuned like an instrument. The music of slowly moving water is more restful than turbulent water, yet the sound should have a certain degree of complexity or it soon becomes monotonous.

More Pitfalls There are other pitfalls: in a garden water should look completely natural; if you want to use it, you must carefully consider its character. Water flows. It has a logical beginning and a logical end, the one being higher than the other. Water that suddenly appears at the top of a pile of rock is unnatural and disquieting. Is this an artesian well? A spring? A geyser like Old Faithful? A leak? Where did it come from?

Unless you live on a very steep slope, a waterfall—that landscaper's favorite—is a natural impossibility. But water needn't plummet to be dramatic. In a stream bed it can swirl and churn with only a slight drop in elevation. A natural-looking stream should

have its source and end hidden from sight so it appears just to have wandered onto the property and then meandered off again.

Fountains have no such constraints because they are obviously man-made and one does not question their source. A fountain generally looks at home in a garden, especially a small one, though it is difficult for it to be anything but a focus of attention.

Pools of water, man-made or natural, are the easiest to fit into a garden and the easiest to live with. Stocked with fish and plants to keep the water clean, they are virtually carefree; though quiet and restful, pools are far from static, sparkling in the sun or rippling when a breeze blows over their surface. However, to make a natural pool look natural is no small trick, and you will find it challenging to disguise the water's edge so it does not look contrived. The giveaway is usually a glimpse of the material lining the pool. The edge must be absolutely level or the lining is going to show above water.

A formal, obviously man-made pool is much easier to build and one tends not to question its rim or source.

Portable Pools Easier still, in fact foolproof, are portable pools. Portable is a relative term because, once filled with water, even the smallest container is too heavy to budge. But the containers are portable when empty and can be moved if the area becomes too shady or otherwise inappropriate. Large pots made of concrete or terra cotta are candidates; so are half-barrels made of oak and sold at nurseries, though these will need plastic liners or a thorough cleaning and soaking to make the staves watertight and to dispel the lingering reek of whisky—their original contents.

There is no minimum size, but

In the author's own garden, a large concrete pot alongside the path contains a fountain. The cord for the submersible pump runs out the drainage hole in the bottom of the container and the hole is sealed with roofing cement. Agapanthus are in the foreground, while a gardenia is the fragrant background. The gray foliage belongs to Jerusalem sage, Phlomis fruticosa. *Little plants are tucked everywhere possible and granite pebbles and stones dignify and harmonize with the plain concrete pavers and pot.*

Almost everything in this fall-planted garden is edible as well as decorative—an intriguingly practical idea. The most colorful plant is an ornamental kale. Other contributors to this vegetable tapestry include red and green lettuces, cabbage, parsley, Swiss chard, and even Brussels sprouts towering in the background. The ornamental kale, for all its beauty, is also edible, by the way.

something about two feet across and nearly as deep will accommodate several fish and any water plant, even water lilies. The fish are necessary to keep mosquitos from breeding in the pool, and they also help with its natural balance, consuming excess algae and plant growth and providing food for the aquatic plants. Ordinary goldfish are the best bet, though little guppy-like mosquito fish may be the only kind able to survive in very small or shallow pools.

A PLACE FOR GOOD TASTES

I confess that in my own garden vegetables have been outnumbered by flowers in an increasing ratio in recent years. I could find beautiful fresh vegetables easily enough at the market but not the flowers I now grow. Still, even in a garden designed to show off flowers in a restful landscape, a place can be found for those edible things that taste so much better homegrown.

Fresh Fruit In particular I am thinking about fruits of all kinds. Blackberries can be trained against a fence and can serve as an ornamental vine. Nothing tastes as wonderful as sun-warmed fresh blackberries. Some of the garden's trees can be fruit trees. Peaches and apricots never reach their full potential of flavor or ripeness at markets; these are fine choices for the garden because they grow on handsome small trees that set out pretty spring flowers.

Be aware that fruits of all kinds have specific climatic needs. In Southern California we are particularly cognizant of this because so many popular fruit varieties—the Elberta peach or Red Delicious apple for instance—will not thrive in our warm winters. They need more chilling (the specific num-

ber of hours when the temperature is below forty-five degrees) than we can provide; but other varieties of the same fruit—the 'Babcock' peach or 'Anna' apple—need less chilling and grow well here. Berries, grapes, and even citrus and other subtropicals have differing requirements, though the limiting factors with them may be whether it gets hot enough to ripen fruit or too cold for their survival.

The great advantage of growing fruit trees or vines is that they almost always serve two functions—as ornamentals and as edibles. Already mentioned is the flowering season of most deciduous fruit trees, because of which some are sold as dual-purpose trees. Fruiting-flowering peaches such as 'Red Baron' are an example. Citrus and many evergreen fruit trees such as loquats or guavas can be used successfully as background plants or, if they are dwarf varieties and are kept neatly clipped they can even become focal points of the garden. Lemon trees have been used as hedges; grape vines can cover trellises as decorative architectural elements.

Herbs Most herbs are decidedly ornamental and many cannot be found fresh at markets. Others are used in the kitchen so often that it is handy to have them growing nearby. Mix them right in with the rest of the flowers and plants in the garden, though it is wise to avoid putting them where insecticides will be sprayed, next to roses, for example.

And Vegetables Most vegetables are a little harder to work into the garden scheme. Though they are, for the most part, ornamental, they are also annuals, large annuals at that, and while they may look great at certain times of the year, at other times they

are too young and small, or past their prime, or their space is empty while you wait for the seasons to change.

Some particularly clever gardeners manage to incorporate vegetables and fruits into the garden nonetheless, though I have managed to find a home in my beds only for strawberries, artichokes, and cardoons, all of which happen to be perennials. The rest of my fruits and vegetables are grown in containers, out of the way while they are coming on but in full view when they are fruiting. Because they are such a sorry sight at markets, hard as rocks and about as tasty, tomatoes always find a home in the garden, though usually in pots.

But see what the designer of the garden pictured here did with vegetables!

A KITCHEN GARDEN

Perhaps the best way of all to use edible plants in the garden is also the oldest: set aside a kitchen garden where fruits, herbs, and vegetables can be grown to perfection. This special place allows you to give them the care and the room they require.

There is no need for the kitchen garden to look any less like a garden than other parts, but because its plants are subject to marked seasonal changes, it is best kept separate. The traditional way to set it apart is with a hedge or low wall as seen in gardens at least since medieval times. Neat raised beds are often used to organize the garden as well as to make the soil warmer and better drained. There is no need to truck in extra soil; the beds will become higher after all the amendments are added that make the earth rich enough for vegetables.

There is only one logical place for a kitchen garden and that is right outside the kitchen. Too often, though, the garden ends up in the back forty where the cook or cook's helper is not likely to make many trips. It is much better, for the sake of your table, to have all the delicious foods you grow as handy to the cook as possible. Kitchen gardens that need daily watching—for pests, for signs of needed water or fertilizer, for exact time of harvest— should be conveniently located.

During their growing period almost all edible plants need a full day of sun, and some could even use a little reflected heat from a wall, so when you plan your kitchen garden, pick a sunny, warm spot. Many vegetables are susceptible to diseases that can be diminished with good air circulation, so pick a spot that is breezy.

Room to Grow Each plant needs a specific amount of space, and one way to plan a kitchen garden is to look up the size of each vegetable (or fruit or herb) and simply draw circles to scale. Cut these out and arrange them as you like, making sure one plant doesn't shade another. To start you on your way, we have drawn some of summer's favorite vegetables. Copy them on stiff paper or cardboard, cut them out, assemble them (they will stand upright like vegetable chess pieces), and then arrange them on a plan of your kitchen garden. The plan should be drawn to a scale of three-quarters inch on paper equals one foot in the garden, the same scale as the vegetable cutouts.

If you want to try growing vegetables mixed in with flowers, or elsewhere in the garden, use these cutouts to experiment with locations. There is even a cutout of a half-barrel container in case you can't find any other place to plant vegetables. It's the perfect size for growing them and can go anywhere in the garden, even on the patio.

Deciduous fruit trees are highly ornamental when in flower, productive when laden with fruit. Some are especially beautiful, such as this 'Red Baron' peach, a special kind of peach called a "fruiting-flowering" variety putting out many more flowers than most. In this case each flower is double with many more petals than normal. The peaches aren't bad either and there is no shortage of them.

A.

KITCHEN GARDEN PLANNER

To make a vegetable garden in miniature, xerox pages 154–157. Glue sheets
to stiff paper and cut pictures out along
broken lines. Some need bases to stand
on, with a slot cut for the tab. The scale
is 3/4 inch to 1 foot. Make a plan of
your garden to the same scale, place
your cutout models on it, moving them
about until the garden layout pleases
you.

On pages 154–155:
A) For the eggplant, make a base
1½ inches in diameter.

B) The sunflower requires a circular
base 1½ inches in diameter.

C) Two pumpkin plants can grow in a 6-
foot diameter circular plot (4½ inches
on model) if you weave their stems
together. Slit semicircles along dotted
lines and hook one over the other.

D) For the red bell pepper, make circular base 3/4 inch in diameter.

E) The row of corn should be folded
vertically down the center into a free-
standing L shape. It holds 16 plants.

On pages 156–157:
F) Cut out the bed of melons and lay it
flat on your plan. Five plants will grow
in this 3 x 12 foot bed.

G) The 12-foot-long trellis made of
welded wire accommodates 11 bean
plants and 5 cucumber vines.

H) A half-barrel planter can hold all
sorts of vegetables. Assemble the
model using tabs provided.

I) Tomatoes grow very well in a circular
cage. Roll the tomato drawing into a
cylinder, fastening with tabs and slots;
insert bottom tabs into a circular base
2¼ inches in diameter.

B.

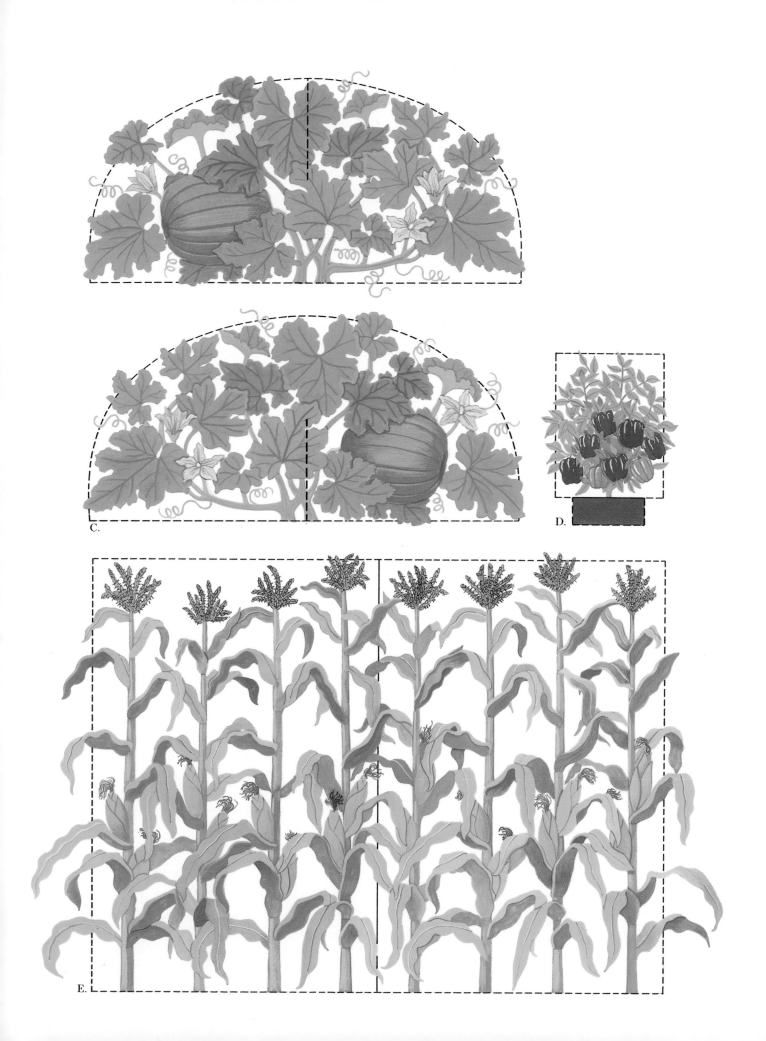

C.

D.

E.

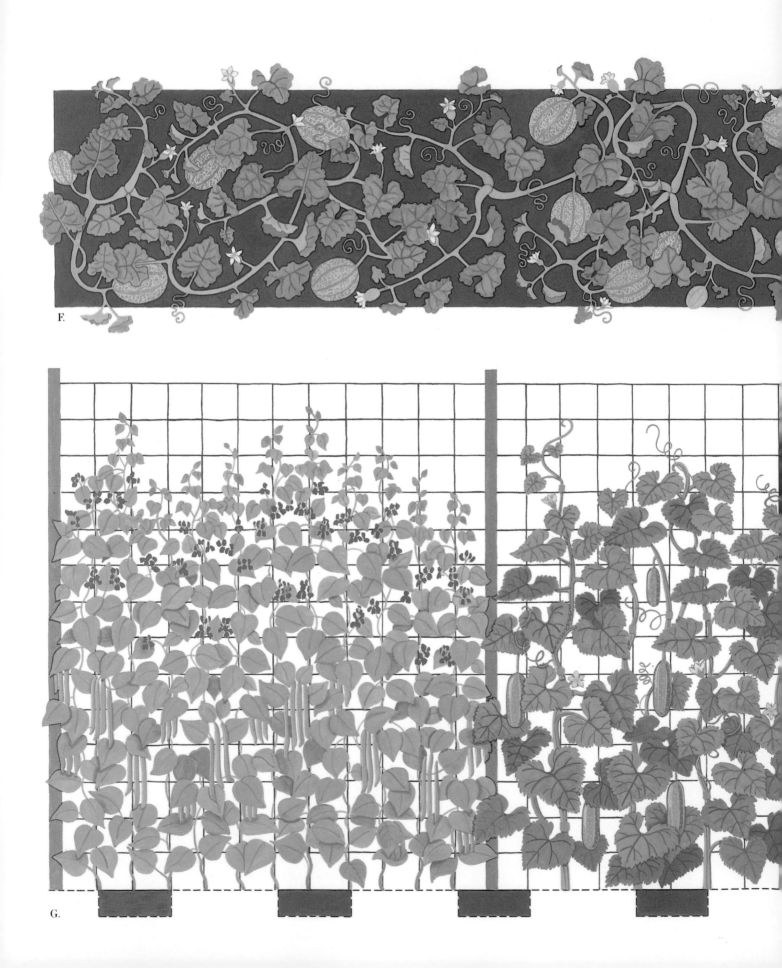

F.

G.

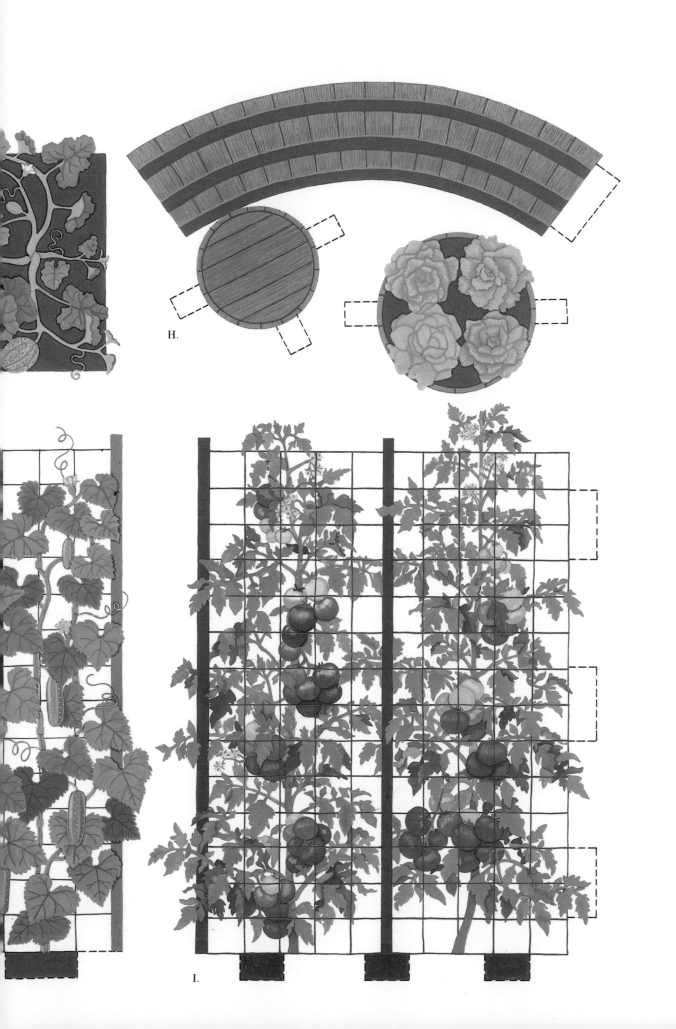

H.

I.

CHAPTER

7

PLANTING
THE
GARDEN

THE IMPORTANCE OF
SOIL PREPARATION

Good gardens have good soil; you need look no further for the secret to their success. And there are no shortcuts. Good soil takes work and time to build, but it is crucial to the successful growing of some of the showier plants.

In planning the garden, we have segregated plants so they grow in special beds, or in borders for flowers and vegetables, or in areas devoted to lawn or ground covers, or as background. Thinking of these areas one at a time, as separate places, helps with the planning process but it also aids with the planting because not all plants need the same kind of soil preparation: some need a great deal, others, somewhat surprisingly, do best without.

Plants That Need Soil Preparation
Flowers (especially perennials) and vegetables, but also lawn grasses and small ground covers—highly productive small plants whose roots grow mostly in the top foot or so of soil—need the most soil preparation. Typically, they grow wild in rich or well-drained soils, and their root systems are not designed to forage far and wide for moisture or nutrients. Another group of plants that need soil preparation are those that might be found growing wild in the woods, including most shade plants such as azaleas and camellias. These expect a soil that is porous and rich with organic matter, such as the leafy soils that make up the forest floor.

Plants That Don't But there is no need to prepare all the soil in a garden. Recent research tends to indicate that trees, shrubs, and shrubby ground covers actually seem to do better when the soil is not tampered with too much.

Their roots are very different from those of smaller plants, being designed to plumb the depths of the earth in search of moisture and nutrients. The roots of a tree can extend a distance four times the spread of its branches, while shrub roots can grow twenty or more feet deep into the ground.

They Need Air Even experienced gardeners sometimes forget the importance of air for roots. They talk about "good drainage," knowing that many plants need a soil that drains excess moisture so it will not become soggy. But what they are really speaking of is air at the roots. A plant's roots need air, just as the leaves do, and as do the soil organisms that help a plant convert raw nutrients into the form it can use. These microorganisms are what makes a soil smell good and seem healthy.

"Good drainage" simply means that there is not so much water in the soil that it excludes air. Water can actually bring air right behind it, if it keeps on moving down through the soil and doesn't rest. You can see in the bathtub what happens in the soil: water running down the drain sucks air in behind it, making that gurgling sound that tells you the tub is empty.

Making "Good Drainage" Rocky and sandy soils are naturally airy, but clay and loam soils are less so, in some cases having no air at all. It's easy enough to test for air—simply dig a hole, fill it with water, and see how long it takes to drain away. If it disappears quickly, you have an airy soil; if it sits for an hour or two you do not.

To make a soil airy you must open up the spaces between the soil particles. Rocky soils and sandy soils are composed of large particles with lots of air spaces already between them, but loam soils have much smaller parti-

The coiled hose, the trowel, the weeding fork, and pruning shears, these homely tools on pages 158–159 symbolize the work and craft of gardening.

A garden begins with the preparation of the soil which is composed of tiny particles. The smallest are the particles in a clay soil, the largest, the particles in a sandy soil. The tiny particles pack closely together, excluding air and water, so a gardener's job is to separate them chemically or physically. A rough turning over of the soil with a spade begins the process.

cles, while clay soils have particles that are essentially invisible with correspondingly little air space between.

You can open up these "heavy" soils chemically or physically, the latter being the most common way because physical amendments solve other problems at the same time. Soil gypsum (sold at nurseries) is a chemical amendment used in California to open up a soil; it chemically binds the particles into larger chunks. But it is only useful in certain soils that are alkaline and made of a heavy clay found in the Southwest. (In other parts of the country, lime is sometimes used instead of gypsum, but never in California because lime is for acid soils in generally high-rainfall areas; California soils are neutral or alkaline.) Soil amendments, such as ground bark or peat moss, have the physical means of separating soil particles; they simply shove aside the particles, providing airy spaces.

Preparing the Soil for Trees and Shrubs Because the roots of trees and shrubs extend over so much territory, it is nearly impossible to effect much change in the soil where they grow. It is best to choose trees and shrubs that grow in your particular kind of soil. If a plant description says it "needs good drainage" and you garden on clay, forget it. Even if you do prepare the soil, the initial success will probably end in eventual failure with the plant dying after it has grown to be quite large.

Instead, plant something that likes the kind of soil you have and do little in the way of preparation. Dig the hole and pile the soil to one side. After planting, put the same soil back in the hole, but pulverize it thoroughly, making sure that there are no large chunks. The fluffed-up soil will improve drainage for those first few critical months. A year later the tree or shrub will not be able to distinguish the soil in the hole from the soil surrounding it so the roots will grow far and wide with no impediment.

Research has shown that roots want to stay in a well-prepared soil and not venture out, like someone under warm covers in a cold house. Since this well-prepared soil is also probably quite rich, the plant grows quickly at first but then falters when the roots become trapped in the planting hole. A tree or shrub planted in soil with little or no preparation, though it might get off to a slower start, will overtake its pampered brother within two years of planting.

A Fluffy Soil for Flowers In nature, flowers tend to grow in the best spots and the best soils, as do grasses and plants used as small ground covers in the garden. These all need the best soil in the garden, one that can be described as being "fluffy."

Flowers need good drainage and a soil that holds moisture near the surface and nutrients. The way to achieve these needs is to add organic matter to the soil. Organic matter may be home-made compost—well-rotted horse or dairy manure (not steer manure), specially treated sawdusts (nitrogen must be added or the organic amendment will steal it from the soil), or peat moss. At first it is best to use something that is available in large quantities; in California, that is usually some mixture of specially treated ground barks and sawdusts, often called RSA for "redwood soil amendment" since they contain redwood sawdust. Later, you can be more creative and find things like mushroom compost (left over from the growing of mushrooms) to further enrich a soil.

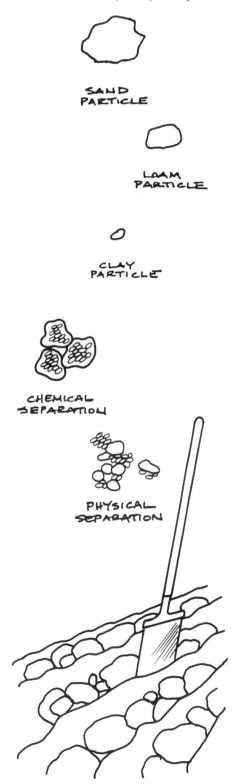

SAND PARTICLE

LOAM PARTICLE

CLAY PARTICLE

CHEMICAL SEPARATION

PHYSICAL SEPARATION

Soil preparation is an ongoing task since the original work gets undone in time. Thoroughly prepare a soil for flowers or vegetables and it makes everything else easier, from weeding to watering.

PREPARING A GARDEN BED

Flowers and vegetables need the best soil, and preparing their beds requires the most time and effort. Lawns and areas of ground cover have to have almost as much work done on their soil, but grass and small plants are neither as demanding or productive as flowers and vegetables. Think of what those last two produce in just a single season! Where do they get the building materials or the energy but from the soil? Because organic matter, such as ground bark and peat moss, acts like little sponges, while also separating the soil particles, they are the preferred amendment (amendment being anything added to the soil). Sand can also separate soil particles and is used for that purpose in potting mixes, but it does not hold onto nutrients or keep moisture in the soil.

Sand Sand can have the reverse of the desired effect as a soil amendment—adding sand to some soils is like adding gravel to cement: it turns it into concrete. Sand can be useful as a soil amendment where you do not want to increase the water- or nutrient-holding ability of a soil—in areas where herbs are to grow "lean" so their oils are more potent, for example. But proceed with caution and experiment first.

Moisture and Nutrients While it may seem odd that we want soil to retain moisture, while at the same time encouraging it to drain quickly, there is really no contradiction. We are just looking for optimum levels of moisture—enough to sustain plant growth for a week or more, but not so much that it excludes air or that the plant drowns. The best soil amendments maintain an optimum balance,

acting as reservoirs and soil separators. They also retain nutrients, those essential plant foods added to the soil as fertilizer. For this reason, amendments are even mixed with sandy soils because sandy soils have little ability of their own to hold onto moisture or nutrients. For all practical purposes, *any* soil that is going to be asked to grow flowers, vegetables, or lawn grasses should be improved with organic amendments.

A Test There is a simple test to see how your soil shapes up, before and after amending it. Squeeze a handful of moist—not wet—soil. If it remains a tight ball, it is a clay that needs amending to increase its airiness. If it crumbles into small chunks you have a good soil, at least as far as its structure is concerned. If it disintegrates into grains, you have a soil with too loose a texture—a sandy or rocky soil—and need to add amendments to increase its ability to hold onto nutrients and moisture.

After you have amended the soil, try the same test and see if it seems better. The best soil for flowers, vegetables, and lawn should crumble into small chunks and feel moist but not sticky or grainy.

And a Formula How much amendment should one add to a garden bed? Probably a truck full, and though it is sold by the bag, it can be ordered more economically by the truckload. Have the amendment piled to one side of the driveway and use a wheelbarrow to add it to the garden as you need it. You will want to add 25 to 50 percent amendment to the soil. If you plan to dig to a depth of a foot, this means adding a four-to-six-inch layer of amendment on top, then mixing it in. That's a lot.

Here is a recipe for preparing a 100-square-foot garden bed—a handy way to figure this all out. Divide all the garden beds into 100-square-foot sections—4 by 25 feet, 10 by 10 feet, 6 by 16½ feet, and so on—so you know how much of each ingredient to buy. Add the following amounts to each 100 square feet of garden bed:

Four three-cubic-foot sacks (a common size) of amendment, or about one-half a cubic yard (truckloads come by the cubic yard).

Two pounds of a complete, all-purpose fertilizer (a one-pound coffee can holds about two pounds of fertilizer).

Ten pounds of gypsum (only in alkaline soils, like California's, that are like a heavy clay).

Mix It In Now comes the work. All the amendment must be mixed smoothly into the soil the way a cook mixes flour and water—there should be no clumps or chunks. The best way is to dig up the garden with a spade after having watered it several days before. The soil should now be moist—not dry or wet—which is the best way to work it. The spade should have a long (eighteen-inch) blade and the blade should be straight. Work across the bed, turning over one row at a time, but don't completely flip the soil over, just turn it on its side. Don't be neat—you are trying to break the soil into big clods that will later be pulverized, and you want to leave a jagged bottom in your trench.

You do not use a rotary tiller at first. That tool digs to a uniform depth and it actually can polish the soil just beneath where it is working. This forms an interface between the soil that is being improved and the untouched, native soil just below, an interface that can block the movement of roots and water.

With the bed dug and rough, spread

Soil preparation in progress. After the soil has been turned with a spade, a small rototiller does an excellent job of mixing in the various amendments. Don't think this is a one-time job. Every few years flower beds such as this, and vegetable gardens as well, require rejuvenation because these prodigious producers use up a soil. At the same time you have the ideal opportunity to divide perennials or move plants to better locations. This is work best done during the cooler times of the year.

Even though there are many new watering devices, it is hard to beat the accuracy and efficiency of the old-fashioned watering basin. That collar of mounded-up soil funnels water directly to the roots of the plants. Here watering basins surround newly planted or recently pruned roses. Watering basins also let you water new plants more often than nearby established plants (which might suffer from too much watering). You simply fill the new plants' basins more often.

the amendments and fertilizer (and gypsum if you are using it) on top of the clods of earth, but note the previous precaution about gypsum. The fertilizer can be any inexpensive brand that contains all three essential nutrients—nitrogen, phosphorus, and potassium—in about equal amounts. It will have numbers like 8-8-8 on the label, or 12-10-10, or something similar. Unless you know what you are doing, avoid fertilizers with a large first number. That first number indicates the amount of nitrogen; too much of it can give plants a chemical burn.

Time for a Tiller Now you can use a rotary tiller (available where gardening equipment is rented) to do the final mixing. You don't need a big unmanageable tiller because the ground has already been roughened and loosened by spading. The nice thing about the tiller is that it is going to thoroughly pulverize the soil and thoroughly mix the ingredients, as an eggbeater would blend flour and water. If you wish, you can do this final mixing with a spade or spading fork, but it will be difficult to break up all the clods completely or to mix the ingredients thoroughly. It will also be more work than you can imagine.

STOMP IT DOWN, WATER, AND WATCH OUT FOR WEEDS

When you have finished adding amendments to the soil, the ground is going to be a lot higher than when you began. By amending, tilling, and digging, you have fluffed up the soil like an eiderdown quilt. This is an advantage because plants are most sensitive to too much water at their crowns— where the roots join the trunk or stem of the plant—and it is impossible for the crowns to get too wet if they are a

few inches above the ground level.

Most likely, however, the bed when amended will be more than a few inches above ground, so you are going to have to stomp it down. It may seem crazy to fluff up the soil and add all those air spaces only to stomp it back down, but you must recompress it or the air spaces are going to be so big and the soil so porous that water will simply run right through and barely dampen the new plants—a soil can be *too* airy. Actually "stomp" may be too strong a word. On lawns, this is done with a big, water-filled roller, but on a garden bed it is enough simply to walk firmly all over the fluffy soil. In time, the soil will settle of its own accord and you can expect it to settle even further after you have stomped it down.

Now Water and Wait Watering will help settle the soil additionally, and rain will do even more. Put a sprinkler on the bed and water it thoroughly; water it several times, in fact, to bring up the weeds whose seeds may be lying in wait. The way to germinate seed is to keep it constantly moist, so for a week or more don't let the bed dry out.

You really want to wait for the weeds to sprout *before you plant*. (This may be the best advice you ever get.) The nearly constant watering is going to sprout the weeds; but because of the muddy ground, it is going to be difficult to enter the bed and get them out if you have already planted flowers.

If before planting you wait two weeks, watering all the time, the weeds will sprout and you can hoe them out in a jiffy. Or spray them with a short-lived herbicide such as Roundup or Kleenup. These work best in warm weather, killing roots and tops. Because these herbicides are short lived, you can plant as soon as the weeds are dead.

kinds of weather. In heavily weed-infested areas, where there are no tree or shrub roots, you might want to invest in having the ground fumigated professionally. That will kill everything, though you must wait to plant for about a month after fumigation. Only fumigation wipes out all the seeds and roots of perennial weeds (such as Bermuda or devil grass). Because it is the nature of weeds to be survivors, they can withstand the most vigorous watering and hoeing; even after such treatment some weeds still remain hidden and waiting for the right time to spring up again.

You will never be completely rid of weeds, but a good start goes a long way toward keeping them in check.

Not the End of It Soil preparation is never finished. It is an ongoing job. Every time an area is replanted, it must be amended again because previous amendments are used up by the plants, or they simply lose their efficacy. You needn't add as much after the original amendment, but at every opportunity you should continue to add to the soil of a flower bed or vegetable garden.

Lawns and ground-cover plantings are another matter. Once they are planted there is little you can do to further improve the soil, other than fertilize. They too will eventually need to be dug up and replanted, though that might take as long as twenty years.

A Possible Exception There is one instance where you might not want to prepare a flower bed in the manner just described: if you are going to grow plants that are native to your area or similar in their demands to native ones. In California, there are many plants that we can grow with little or no

water beyond the regular rainfall. For these plants the beds are perhaps best left with little or no soil preparation other than digging and tilling it. Adding organic amendments would increase the drainage of the soil, but that would also mean you must water more often because amended soil is more porous than natural soil and the water runs right through it—this is true, at least, in the case of clay soils, our most common kind.

The catch is: You must be very careful about watering in summer because if you do the soil will be unnaturally damp for that time of the year. Native and other drought-tolerant plants should be watered their first year in the ground while they are becoming established, but then irrigation should be as infrequent as once a month. Avoid watering in August altogether, or you will encourage root rots that thrive in moist, warm soil.

DIGGING A HOLE AND OTHER PERTINENT PLANTING INFORMATION

Trees and shrubs are the easiest to plant because they require the least soil preparation, even though the hole you plant them in must be big. Some new research suggests that you dig this hole in a new fashion: to avoid any kind of "interface" where two different kinds of soil come together like a solid wall. You do not want the hole to be neat, but rather to have a jagged surface so the roots cannot become confused and begin circling round and round as they often do inside a nursery container.

The hole need not be deep. Dig it just deep enough so the plant can rest on a pedestal of solid ground after planting and so it will not settle. You don't want it to settle, or in time its

Lots of Weeds? If you are starting a garden bed or lawn in an area where a great many weeds grew or are still growing, it's better to back up a little and take care of them before preparing the soil. Again, Roundup or Kleenup are the most frequently used herbicides, but you must follow the directions carefully since they work only under some conditions and in certain

crown is likely to become buried, making it very susceptible to all sorts of fatal rots and diseases.

The hole should be wide, however, about three times as wide as the root ball. On either side of the solid pedestal, dig a little deeper so the roots have a place to go; in the bottom of this circular trench put a complete fertilizer. It should look something like the drawings on page 166.

Remember not to add amendments to the dirt that you shovel back into the hole, just pulverize it so there are no clods or chunks, and gently tamp it down with your foot as you fill.

Root-bound Plants Watch out for plants that are root-bound. This means that the roots have begun to circle inside the nursery container or to collect at its sides or bottom. They must be untangled and straightened out, and if they have become completely matted you may have to pull or cut some off to give them a fresh start. If this is necessary, you should also cut off some small branches in order not to overburden the remaining roots. The plant will quickly recover. After untangling the roots, drape them over the sides of the pedestal in the planting hole.

You must also watch out for root-bound plants in garden beds, but you can dig an ordinary hole because all of the soil has been prepared. Planting in your rich and fluffy new soil will be a treat. Around new plants be sure to press down the soil firmly with your hands, or it will be so loose that the water will simply flow around and past the new plants' roots.

Can't Water Too Much At first you almost can't water too much. The roots have yet to grow out into the soil, and it is hard to keep that root ball moist, but after a few weeks, as the roots begin to

spread into the new soil, the watering should begin to taper off. The first year make sure the plant has adequate water at all times, but after that it should be established well enough to get by on a minimum. After the plant has had a year in the ground, it is far more important to let the soil dry a little between irrigations or rains so it does not rot from too much moisture.

Bare-Root Planting There is another way to plant and that is "bare root." Bare-root plants are just that—they are sold while dormant with no soil around their roots. In California, it is the favored way to plant roses, deciduous fruit trees, and even some deciduous ornamental trees such as birch; the time to plant is short—January and February.

Many believe that planting bare root is the best way, although it is possible only with the few plants sold like that. A problem with planting anything grown in a container is that the roots have been restricted and are not growing in a natural fashion—they are growing around in a circle instead of spreading out. Planting bare root lets you position the roots so they can continue to reach out into the soil and you can be sure that they are not pot-bound.

It is best to buy bare-root plants that have been kept in bins filled with damp sawdust, but instead, most nurseries sell them with their roots wrapped in plastic bags. When you buy them wrapped in this fashion, you are gambling that the roots are alive and healthy, not dry, or (more likely) rotted. If the roots are the least bit dry, they should be soaked overnight in a pail of water to plump them up. If they are rotted, they will feel squishy, and if you cut the roots, the inside will not be white but off-color. Reject them!

How you dig a hole would seem to be one of those things that never change, but recent research has shown there is a better way. The idea is to dig a hole in which the plant's roots will not become trapped. So make the sides of the hole slope away from the center to encourage roots to grow out and away from the plant (upper left).

It is also important that the plant not settle into the soil after planting, so leave a pedestal of undisturbed soil for the plant to sit on (center left).

Bare-root plants go in a similar hole but their roots should be spread over a cone of soil mounded up in the bottom (lower left).

Staking is a regrettable practice because it adds little to the aesthetic quality of a garden. But staking is absolutely necessary for tall flowers such as delphiniums. Stakes should go in the ground at planting time so they do not disturb the growing roots later on. Tie the plant directly to the stake with something soft and flexible. Trees and other large plants should not be staked this way; they should be tied between two sturdy stakes placed about a foot on either side of the trunk. This allows them to sway in every breeze and develop strength. Tied tightly to a stake, they lose strength, like an arm confined in a cast.

Enough Roots? You are also gambling that there are enough roots. Many roots are lost when the plant is dug from the field, but there should still be a good number. If there aren't, consider taking the plant back to the nursery in exchange for another. A few nurseries are now potting up their bare-root plants. They see it as a compromise solution. If you plant immediately, you can simply shake the soil off the roots and plant it bare root; if you can't get around to it right away and wait too late in the bare-root season, the plant will be able to root into the potting mix in the container, and then you can plant it as if it were container-grown.

With bare-root plants, never let the roots dry out completely, but also never let them soak for longer than overnight. They should be plump with moisture before being planted, and it is best to keep them out of the sun for the first few days. Spread the roots out, then dig a hole a little wider than the spread of the roots. In the bottom of this hole mound up a cone of soil to set the plant on. This cone supports the plant and lets you arrange the roots so they are all heading in the right direction—down and out.

Sprinkle a little fertilizer in the bottom of the hole and cover it with an inch of soil. You can add soil amendments to the dirt that will be put back in the hole, or you can simply put the soil back in the hole after first pulverizing it. There is some debate about which is the better way. Do not fill the hole with soil that is wet or full of clods. Some gardeners sieve it through a quarter-inch screening to make sure it is not lumpy. It's very important that the soil be pulverized and fine and that it be firmed down as it is put back in the hole. You want to avoid any large air spaces next to the roots. After

filling the hole, mound up soil in a ring around its circumference to make a basin, then thoroughly soak the soil.

WATERING WISDOM, STAKING, AND MULCHING

Water is a precious resource in California where gardeners should use it prudently. Trees and background plantings of shrubs, large-scale ground covers, and other utilitarian plantings should be chosen for their ability to survive with little water. Water should be saved for the flower beds and the vegetable garden, and these should be watered with care.

Much of the water we put on the garden is wasted by evaporation. The trick is to wean plants from a regimen of frequent watering to watering less and less often but more thoroughly each time. Let the water run awhile so it soaks deep into the soil. There it is safe from evaporation, a waiting reservoir for plant roots.

Though many people think they must water every few days, it is quite possible to water less than once a week, even in the southern half of the state, if when you water you do so thoroughly. Then, before watering again, check with a spade or soil probe to see if the soil is dry several inches down, and water only if it is. In time, you will develop an instinct for when to water.

When you first plant, you must water often because the plants haven't tapped into the soil yet. During the first few weeks, it is almost impossible to overwater, but after that, begin the weaning process. Later in a plant's life overwatering is a definite danger and the leading cause of plant mortality.

Fertilizing Is No Mystery Feeding plants or, more properly, fertilizing them, is easy if you do not get confused by the multiplicity of products made for the job. All you really need to add to most California soils—after initially preparing the soil—is nitrogen, which is the first of the three numbers on a package of fertilizer—the 10 in the 10-8-8 formula found on the package label. The other elements should be added whenever you are planting or preparing a soil, otherwise they are of minor importance since they cannot move down in the soil, even in liquid form. They must be down where the roots are from the beginning.

But nitrogen does move in the soil. In fact, it moves right on through a soil, beyond and beneath the plant roots so it needs to be added regularly. It is the element most responsible for growth. Always use products that are high in nitrogen, fertilizers with numbers like 14-0-0, 16-8-8, 10-8-8, or something similar. Do be aware that very high nitrogen fertilizers, with numbers like 24-0-0, can burn plants if used improperly, so apply them precisely according to instructions.

If fertilizers still seem mysterious, simply buy a product labeled as an all-purpose granular fertilizer, scatter it among the plants, and use a sprinkler to water it into the soil.

Container Exceptions Plants grown in containers are the exception to many of the rules previously mentioned. They probably should be watered every few days, or even every day in hot weather, and they need to be fertilized often—every few weeks—with a fertilizer that has all the necessary elements since the plants are growing in an artificial soil. It is easiest to buy potting soil by the bag and extend it by adding one-third to one-half natural soil. You will also have to water less often with this mixture.

Staking Staking plants is something to avoid if possible—but often it is not possible. Some plants just won't stand up by themselves, delphiniums being an example. So if you plant delphiniums, foxgloves, or other tall plants, put stakes in the ground at the same time to avoid damaging the roots later.

Mulching The last step, and one that is optional, is to cover the bare ground around plants with a mulch of some kind. In the flower garden mulch keeps rain and sprinklers from splashing mud up onto the foliage, and helps keep down weeds, though it may also encourage all sorts of bugs. These include earwigs and cutworms as well as their predators, such as ground beetles or stinkbugs. Mulches also help regulate changes in soil temperature from day to day. They can be a problem if kept too moist, for plants will make roots in the mulch when they should be rooting much deeper. The ideal is a mulch of medium-sized organic matter (about the size of the pieces that come out of a compost shredder), piled about two-to-three inches deep and kept dry with infrequent watering. Plastic and other artificial mulches are best to use in the vegetable garden where appearance isn't so important. What does matter is not to encourage bugs: there is nothing worse than finding a head of lettuce full of earwigs.

THE ZIGS AND ZAGS OF GARDENING

Many people have the idea that the road to a good garden is straight—you come up with a plan, plant accordingly, and then wait for everything to mature. You expect to do a little weeding and tidying up from time to time, and there will be tempting new plants each spring, but otherwise you are finished—the garden is complete.

In fact, a gardener's course contains many zigs and zags. Something grows too big, or is the wrong color, or up and dies. A path is in the wrong place or a patio gets too much or too little sun. What is more, your taste is sure to change as you discover plants you didn't know about or after you see what others have done in their gardens. While my intent in telling you this is to forewarn you of these zigs and zags, I do not want to sound the least bit discouraging since the ever-changing nature of a garden is one of its most charming attributes. Gardening is an ongoing affair, changing with the seasons and the years. It is never static and you are never done. A garden is always alive and growing and so should be the gardener.

In my own garden I have moved one azalea seven times trying to find the perfect place. I have excitedly ripped up entire sections to make room for newly discovered plants. A favorite tree died but the resulting vacancy left an unexpected sunny spot for flowers. The central path has been added to and subtracted from to afford a better flow through the plantings (and to make room for a wheelbarrow at one point). After discovering how wonderful a small bed of flowers and ornamental grasses looked when back-lit by the sun, I even moved a patio and bench so they could overlook this sunny scene.

You do not want to tear up paths and patios too often, however, and the guidelines in this book should help give the garden a solid backbone to begin with. But do not be afraid to make changes when necessary. Look forward to them, because with every change comes experience, knowledge, awareness, satisfaction, and growth.

Some of the basic tools of gardening: A straight-bladed spade for turning soil and dividing plants, kept sharp with a bastard file; a small trowel and fork for planting, loosening soil, and weeding; pruning shears, including the long-bladed Corona No. 5, a favorite for cutting back perennials; a little container with a granular fertilizer to add to the soil when planting or cultivating; measuring spoons; plant tags on which to write the name of a plant and when it was planted. Without this last bit of information, you cannot really learn what you are growing and when to expect it. Names are important for the growth of the garden—and the gardener.

INDEX

Page numbers in *italics* refer to captions.

Abutilons, *72*, 73
   A. pictum 'Thompsonii,' *63*
Acanthus, 90
Accent, 57, *57*
Accessories for the garden, 138–139
Achillea, see Yarrow
Acid soils, 72, 161
African daisies, 118
African marigolds, 124
Agapanthus, 64, *97, 99*, 132, *149*
Aggeleler & Musser, 103
Air and air circulation
   cold air, 18, *19*
   for kitchen gardens, 153
   and roominess, 54
   and soil preparation, 160–161
   through fences, 74
   winds, 19
Ajuga, 91, 138
Alchemilla, 15
   A. pectinate, *14*
Algerian ivy, 75
Alkaline soils, 161, 163
Aluminum sulfate, 72
'Amabel Landsell' camellias, *69*
Amendments, *see* Soil amendments
American marigolds, 124
Ammonium phosphate, 64
Anemones, *63, 100*
'Angelique' tulips, *100*
'Anna' apple trees, 150
Annuals
   with bulbs, *100*, 110
   colors of, 91, *100*
   in flower beds, 88
   foliage of, 90
   proper use of, 100–101
Anthemis, *63*
'Apricot Beauty' tulip, 111, *111*
Apricot trees, 150
Artemisia, *123*
Artichokes, 153
Atriums, 18
Aucubas, 73
Australian violet, 143
'Autumn Gold' ginkgo, 81
Avocado trees, 78
Azaleas, 70–71, *71*, 72–73, *78*, 160
Azure Blue pansies, *106*

'Babcock' peach trees, 150
Bachelor's buttons, 68, *116*
Backgrounds, *46*, 46–47, 53
   hedges, fences, and walls for,
      73–74
   shrubs for, 65–66
   trees for, 77
      fruit trees, 150

Balance in design, 56
Bambini pansies, 104
Bamboo poles, *144*
Banana belts, 18–19, *19*
Banning, Joan, 50
Bare-root planting, *167*, 167–168
Bark, 161
Bastard files, *171*
Bays for annuals, 101
Beaconsfield pansies, 104, *104*
Beans, 154
Bearded iris, *48*, 88
Bedding begonias, *138*
Bedding nicotiana, 126
Begonias, 60, *138*, 145
'Belle of Portugal' climbing rose, 75
Beloperone guttata, 134
Benches, *26*, 32, 139
Bermuda grass, 38, 166
Berry, Mark, 31, 32
Better Gardens (nursery), 103
Biennials, 101
Birch trees, *21*, 110, 111, 167
Bird-of-paradise, *78*
Bird's eyes gilia, 118, *119*
Blackberries, 150
Black Knight delphiniums, 61
Blue agapanthus, 132
Blue-bedder salvia, 124
Blue fescue, *95*, *131*, 132
Blue Fountain delphiniums, 63–64
Bluegrass, 38
Bluejay delphiniums, 60
Blue star creeper, *41*, *127*
Blue thimble-flower, 118
Bonsai, 70
Borkovetz, Richard, 118
Borrowed landscape, 46
Borum, Ruth, 94
Boston ivy, 75
Bottlebrush tree, *50*
Bougainvillea, 12, *13*
Boulders, 138–139
Branches of trees, 77
Breezes, 19
Bricks, *35*, 50
Bristol, W. M., 107
Bromeliads, 145
Brussels sprouts, *150*
Bulbs, 88, 108, 112–114
   under birch trees, *21*
   cultivation of, 108–109
   in flower beds, 88, *100*
   location of, 108
   and pansies and violas, 107
   planting of, *111*
   see also specific plants, e.g., Daffodils;
      Ranunculus; Tulips
Burbank, Luther, 60
Butterflies, 139

Cabbage, *150*
Cages, for tomatoes, 154
Calendulas, 101
California
   alkaline soils of, 163
   annuals in, 100
   bare-root planting in, 167
   bulbs in, 108
   camellias in, 68
   climate in, 18
   colors in, 123
   delphiniums in, 60
   dianthus in, 93
   fertilizers needed in, 169
   foxgloves in, *91*
   gypsum used in, 161
   hydrangeas in, 72
   microclimates of slopes in, 18
   organic soil amendments in, 161
   pansies and violas in, 103
   perennials in, 91
   ranunculus in, *108*
   roses in, 89
   shrubs for, 66, *67*
   soil preparation in, 166
   watering in, 166, 168
   white heliotropes in, 128
   see also Southern California
California Garden Flowers (book), 103, 107
California Giants zinnias, 100
'California Gold' bougainvillea, *12*
California pepper tree, *78*
California poppies, 100, 115, 118, *119*
California redwood, 81
Calla lily 'Green Goddess,' 134, *135*
Camellias, 68, *69*, 72–73, 160
Candytuft, *88*, *99*, 99
Cannas, *32*
Canterbury bells, *63*, 68, 101
Cape Cod Weeder, 143
Cardoons, 90, 153
Carnations, *see* Dianthus
Carolina laurel cherry, 66, *67*
Catharanthus rosea, 99
Chain-link fences, 76
Checkerboard hedge, *26*, 40
Cheilanthes fendleri, *138*
Chia, 115
'Chimes' iris, *123*
Chrysanthemums, 61, 99, 110
   C. multicanle, 99
   C. paludosum, *99*, 99, 126, 146
Cinerarias, 68, *100*, 101
Citrus trees, *53*, 128, 150
City gardens, 140, *141*
Claremont, California, 118
Clay soils, 160–161, *161*, 163
Clear Crystal violas, 104
Clematis, 76
Climate

for annuals, 100–101
in California, 18
and light, 21
planning for, 17–19
Climbing roses, *13*, 75, *88*
Cold air, 18, *19*
Collectibles, 145
Colors, 123–135
    of abutilons, 73
    of annuals, 101
        vs. perennials, 91
    and backgrounds, *53*
    blue, 124
    for entry walk, 12
    of ginkgo leaves, 81
    gray foliage, *123*, 126, *127*, 130–133, *131*
    green flowers, 126, 134, *135*
    of hydrangeas, 72–73
    and light, 19
    with pansies and violas, 107
    pink, 124
    red-through-blue group and orange-through-
        yellow group, 124
    of Satsuki azaleas, 71
    for shrubs in background, 53
    white, 124–126, 128–129
    yellow and orange, 124
Columbines, *63*, *88*, *91*, *95*, 110
Compacted earth, 35
    see also Decomposed granite
Compost, 161
Concrete for paving, 35
Connelly, Kevin, 115, 116, *116*, 117
Containers for plants
    problems with, 167
    vegetables in, 153
    watering and fertilizers in, 169
    wooden troughs at Parklabrea, 146, *147*
    see also Half-barrels; Pots
Coral bells, *85*, *88*, *91*, 110, *127*
Coreopsis, *26*, *53*, *58*, 110
Corn, 154
Corona No. 5 shears, 97, *171*
Corsican hellebore, 134, *135*
Creepers, *41*
Creeping fig, 75
Creeping oregano, 143
Crocuses, 111
    C. goulimyi, 138
    saffron, 112–113, *113*
Crystal Bowl violas, 104, *106*, 107
Crystal Palace lobelia, 146
Cucumbers, 154
Cutting back
    of pansies and violas, 107
    of perennials, 97
Cutworms, 171
Cypress, *36*, 57

Daconil (fungicide), 107
Daffodils, 61, 107, 108, 109
Dairy manure, 161
'Dai-Shu-Hai' Satsuki azaleas, *71*
Daisies, *see* African daisies; English daisies;
    Gloriosa daisies; Santa Barbara daisies;
    Shasta daisies
Date palms, 78
Dawn redwood, 81, *81*
Daylilies, *35*, *63*, *88*
Deciduous trees, 110, *153*, 167
Decomposed granite (d.g.), *29*, 32, *36*, 40, 50, 118
Delphiniums, *53*, 57, 60–64, *63*, 91, *91*, 110, 129,
    168, 171
    D. cardinale, 64
Descanso Gardens, 81
Design, *see* Planning

Devil winds, *see* Santa Ana winds
d.g., *see* Decomposed granite
Dianthus, 64, 68, *85*, 88, *92*, *93*, *124*, *133*, 143
Digging holes, 166–167, *167*
Division of perennials, 97, *97*
Dogwoods, 110
'Donnan's Dream' camellias, *69*
Dormancy of perennials, 97
Doronicum, 63
'Double Delight' roses, *99*, 130
Drainage, 160–161
Drawing plans, 16
Drip emitters, 40
Drought-resistant plantings, *36*
Drymondia, 143
Dusty miller, *127*, *131*, 133
Dwarf agapanthus, 99
Dwarf eugenia, 138
Dyer, Janet, 118
Dyer, Steven, 118
Dyssodia, 124

Earwigs, 171
Eastern redbuds, 78
Eaves of house, 18
Edible plants, *150*, 150–153
    see also Fruit; Herbs; Vegetables
Eggplants, 154
'Elizabeth Campbell' phlox, 61
English daisies, *88*, 101
English gardens
    colors in, 123
    flowers in, 85, 86, 90
        dianthus, 92
        lamb's ears, 131
English lavender, *131*
Entry walk, 11–12
Environmental Seed Producers, 115
Epiphytic plants, 145
'Esther Read' Shasta daisy, *129*
Eucalyptus trees, 78
Eugenias, *85*, 138
Euphorbias, 134
    E. wulfenii, 134, *135*
Evans, Bill, 38
Evergreen magnolias, 77

'Fairmount' ginkgo, 81
Farewell-to-spring, 100
Fast growth
    of delphiniums, 64
    of marguerites, 110
    of shrubs, 65
    of trees, 78
Felix pansies, 107
Fences, 73–74, *75*
    as backgrounds, 46, 53
    and cold air, 18
    gaps in, 74
    for vines, 76
Ferns, 68, *138*, 145
Fertilizer, 168–169
    amount of, 163
    and bare-root planting, 168
    for camellias, 68
    container for, *171*
    in containers for plants, 169
    mixing of, with soil, 164
    Osmocote fertilizer, 64
    for perennials, 97
Fescues, 38, *41*, *95*
    blue fescue, *95*, *124*, *131*, 132
Festuca 'Bronzeglanz,' 132
Festuca ovina glauca, 124
    see also Blue fescue
Feverfew, 126

Files, 171
Fish, 14, 150
'Flamingo' dianthus, *93*
Flax, *14*
Fletcher, Robert, 40, *127*
Flower beds, 86–91, 94, *95*
    annuals in, 101
    Blue Fountain delphiniums in, 64
    for bulbs, 109–110
    grandstanding with, 98–99
    size of, 86, *86*
Flower borders, 86
    camellias in, 68
    delphiniums in, 61
    dianthus in, 93
    lamb's ears in, 132
Flowerland (nursery), 103
Flowers, 85–118
    on abutilons, 73
    and background, 65
    on fruiting-flowering trees, *153*
    and light, 19–21
    and shade, 21
    on shrubs, 54
    and soil preparation, 160, 161–162
    from vines, 76
    see also Colors; Flower beds; Flower borders;
        specific kinds, e.g., Azaleas; Camellias;
        Delphiniums; Roses
Flue-tile planters, 140, *141*
Foam balls, for practice in composition, *55*
Foam-core, *16*, 17
Focal points
    accents as, 57
    in formal gardens, *29*, 29–30
    benches as, 32
    fruit trees as, 150
    in gardens without lawns, 42
    pots as, 145
    straddlestones as, 48
Foliage
    of bulbs, 108
    in flower beds, 90
    and forcing the perspective, 57
    gray, *123*, 126, *127*, 130–133, *131*
    of perennials, 91
Follies, 58
Forcing the perspective, 57
'Forest Pansy' Eastern redbud, 78
Forget-me-nots, *100*
Formal gardens
    balance in, 56
    paths in, 26–29, *30*
    with roses, *30*, 31–32
    surprise in, 57
Foundation planting, 47
Fountain grass, *43*
Fountains, 140, *141*, 149, *149*
Foxgloves, *91*, 101, 171
Freesias, 114
French marigolds, 124
Frost, 18
Fruit, 150
    of ginkgoes, 81
    see also Fruit trees
Fruiting-flowering trees, *153*
Fruit trees, 61, *153*, 167
Fumigation of soil, 166
Fungicides, for pansies and violas, 107
Fungus, of pansies and violas, 104–107
Furniture, 139

Galahad delphiniums, 61
Gardenias, 128, *149*
Garden pinks, *see* Dianthus
Gazanias, *131*

Gazebos, 42
Gennaro, George de, 109, *111*
Geraniums, *138*, 146, *147*
Ginkgoes, *46*, 81, *81*
Gloriosa daisies, 124
Godetia, 100
Golden fleece, 124
Goldfish, 150
Grandstanding, 98–99
Grape ivy, *138*
Grape vines, 150
Grasses, *36*, *43*, 161
   see also Lawns
Gravel, *35*, *36*
Greene, Isabelle, *131*
'Green Goddess' calla lily, 134, *135*
Green lettuce, *150*
Gromulch, 64
Ground bark, 161
Ground beetles, 171
Ground covers, 40, *41*, *127*, 138, 160, 161, 166, 168
Growth of plants, *see* Fast growth; Size; Slow
    growth
Guava trees, 150
'Gudoshnik' tulips, 111, *111*
Guffey, Mary Ellen, *100*
Guinevere delphiniums, 61
Gypsum, 161, 163, 164

Half-barrels
   for pools, 149
   for vegetables, 153, 154
Hanging baskets, 107
Heat
   and bulbs, 109
   and ground covers, 40
   for kitchen gardens, 153
Hedges
   as background, 53
   checkerboard hedge, *26*, 40
   for kitchen gardens, 153
   lemon trees as, 150
   proper creation of, 73
   star jasmine for, *32*, *32*
Helichrysum petiolatum, 12
Heliotrope, 128, *129*
Hellebore, 134, *135*
Helleborus lividus corsicus, *see* Corsican hellebore
Herbaceous perennials, 91
Herbicides, 116, 164–166
Herbs, 144, 150, 162
Heuchera maxima, *127*
Hills, *see* Slopes and hills
Holes, digging of, 166–167, *167*
Hollyhocks, 57, *58*
'Honor' rose, 129
Horse manure, 161
Hoses, *161*
House
   view of, from garden, 47
   see also North side of house; South side of house
Howard, Paul J., 103
Huntington Botanical Garden, *131*
Hyacinths, 109
Hybridizing
   of delphiniums, 60
   of pansies, 103
Hydrangeas, *72*, 72–73

Iberis, 99
'Iceberg' roses, *85*, *91*, 129, *129*
Iceland poppies, 21, *88*, *91*, 101
Ice plants, 99, 118, *119*
Impatiens, 22, *22*, 101, 110, *138*
Imperial Blue pansies, 104
Imperial Orange Prince pansies, 104

Informal gardens, *32*, 33–34
   paths in, 26, 30, *30*, *35*
'Inspiration' climbing rose, 88
Iochroma cyaneum, 14
Irises, 48, 62, *88*, 111, *111*, *123*
Italian cypress, *36*, 57
Ivy, *29*, *48*, 50, 75, *138*
Ivy geranium, 146

Japanese aucuba, 73
Japanese gardens, paths in, 26
Japanese privet, 66, *67*
Japonica camellias, 68
Jasmine, 128
'Jealousy' dianthus, *133*
Jekyll, Gertrude, 14, 85, 130
Jerusalem sage, *149*
Johnny-jump-up, 104, *106*
Johnson, Hugh, 26
Justicia brandegeana, 134
   J. b. 'Chartreuse,' *135*

Kale, *150*
Kees, Karen, 33
'Kickoff' camellias, 69
King Arthur delphiniums, 61
'King George' Johnny-jump-up, *106*
'King Henry' Johnny-jump-up, 104
Kinnock, Beryl, 146
Kinnock, Ronnie, 146
Kitchen gardens, 153–157
Kleenup (herbicide), 116, 164, 166

"Lace-cap" hydrangeas, *72*
Lady Banks rose, *50*
'Lady Forteviat' climbing rose, *88*
Lamb's ears, *91*, *127*, 130–132, *133*
Lancelot delphiniums, 61
Lantana, 129, *129*
Larkspur, 68, 101
Laurentia fluviatilis, *see* Blue star creeper
Laurustinus, 66, *67*
Lavender, 12, *14*, 85, *131*
Lawns, 36–40
   absence of, 42
   with ginkgoes, 81
   between sidewalk and flowers, 98–99
   and soil preparation, 160, 166
   and trees, 78
Leaves
   of trees, 78
   see also Foliage
Lemon trees, 150
Le Nôtre, André, 30
Lettuce, *150*
Licorice plant, 12
Light, *see* Sunlight
Ligustrum japonicum, *see* Japanese privet
Ligustrum vulgare, 66
Lilies, 111
   see also Calla lily 'Green Goddess'; Daylilies
Lilium speciosum 'Rubrum,' 63
Lime, 161
Linaria, 101
Loam soils, 160–161
Lobelia, *88*, 99, *99*, *124*, 146, *147*
Location
   of annuals, 101
   of bulbs, 108
   of kitchen gardens, 153
   for pansies and violas, 107
   planning for, 17–19
   of pots, 144–145
   see also Backgrounds; Planning; Shadows and
    shade; Sunlight
Logee's Greenhouses, 128

Loquat trees, 150
Lychnis, *14*, 130
   L. coronaria 'Alba,' 132

Madagascar jasmine, 75–76
Magnolias, 77, 78, 111
Majestic Giants pansies, 103
Maltese cross, 132
Mandevilla 'Alice du Pont,' 76
Manure, 161
Marguerites, *99*, 110
Marigolds, *99*, 100, 124
Matterhorn freesias, 114
McLaren, John, 103
Measuring spoons, *171*
Melons, 154
'Mermaid' climbing rose, *13*
Metasequoia, 81
   see also Dawn redwood
Mexican evening primrose, *14*, *58*, *123*
Mexico, annuals from, 100
Microclimates, 18
Miller, Hortense, *58*
'Miss Lingard' phlox, 63
Model making, *16*, 17
Moisture, *see* Soils, moisture in; Watering
Moody Blues pansies, 104
'Moonshine' yarrow, 132
Mosquito fish, 150
Mosquitos, 150
Mounding, 12
   and paths, *29*, 30
Mulch, 171
   for ground covers, 40
   of pebbles, 138
   for plants between paving stones, 143
Mums, *see* Chrysanthemums
Mushroom compost, 161
Myrthus communis, 66
Myrtles, 66, *67*

Narcissus, 111
Nasturtiums, *88*
Nectarine trees, 109–110
Nemesia, 63
New Zealand flax, *14*
Nicke, Walt, 143
Nicotiana, 61, *126*, *135*
Nitrogen, 161, 164, 169
North side of house, 19, *72*
   camellias for, 68
   Corsican hellebore for, 134
   'Green Goddess' calla lily for, 134
   microclimate of, 18
Nuccio's Nurseries, 70

Oakland Spring Flower Show, 60
Olive tree, *100*
Open spaces, 36–40
   see also Lawns; Patios; Roominess
'Orange King' bougainvillea, 12, *13*
Orchids, 145
Oregano, 143
Ornamental kale, *150*
Ortho Multipurpose Fungicide, 107
Osmocote fertilizer, 64
Oxalis, *113*, 114
   O. purpura Grand Duchess, 113–114

Pacific Coast iris 'Chimes,' *123*
Pacific Giant delphiniums, 60–61, *61*, 64
Palos Verdes stones, *14*, *14*
Pansies, *99*, 101, 103–107, *104*, 104–107
Parklabrea (Los Angeles), 146
Parsley, *150*
Paths, *26*, 26–30

entry walk, 11–12
in formal gardens, 26–30
in informal gardens, 33–34, *35*
as open space, *43*
planning of, 16, 38
and plants between paving stones, 142–143
see also Paving
Patios, *13*, *22*, 38–40, 50, *138*, 146
Paving, 35–36, 40
plants with, 142–143, *143*
see also Decomposed granite
Peach trees, 63, 109, 150
see also 'Red Baron' peach trees
Peat moss, 64, 71, 161
Pebbles, 138–139, 140
Pennisetum setaceum 'Rubrum,' *43*
'Penny' dianthus, 93, *93*
Penstemon, *53*, 63, *95*, *124*
Perennials
with bulbs, 110
division and dormancy of, 97
for flower beds, 91, *100*
and soil preparation, 160
Perspective in design, 56–57
Petal blight of camellias, 68
Petunias, *63*
Phlomis fruticosa, 149
Phlox, *32*, *99*, 146
'Elizabeth Campbell,' 61
'Miss Lingard,' 63
Phosphorus, 164
Pinks, *see* Dianthus
Pittosporum tobira, 54
P. t. 'Variegata,' 73
see also 'Wheeler's Dwarf' pittosporum
Placement, *see* Location
Planning
of backgrounds, 46–47
with shrubs, 65–66
beginning of, 16–17
and climate and location, 17–19
of flowers, 85–119
and light, 19–21
of paths, 26–30
rules of design for, 54–58
of shadows and shade, 21–22
of trees, 76–78
of water in the garden, 149–150
see also Air and air circulation; Climate; Colors;
Fast growth; Focal points; Formal gardens;
Location; Size; Slow growth
Planters, *see* Containers for plants
Planting, 160–171
of perennials and bulbs, 110
of wildflowers, 116–118
see also Air and air circulation; Fertilizer; Heat;
Location; Roominess; Soils; Sunlight;
Watering; Weeds and weeding; specific
plants
Plastic mulches, 171
Pools, 10, 12, *13*, 149–150
Poppies, *116*
see also California poppies; Iceland poppies;
Shirley poppies
Portulaca, 144
Potassium, 164
Potato vine, 76
Pots, *144*
for annuals, 101
with fountains, *149*
for pansies and violas, *104*
placement of, 144–145
for pools, 149
Potting soil, 169
Power, Nancy Goslee, 11, 14, 15, 40
Primroses, *48*, 68, *100*, 111

see also Mexican evening primrose
'Pristine' rose, 129
Privets, 66
Proportion in design, 56
Pruning, 53, 73
see also Cutting back
Pruning shears, *161*, *171*
Prunus, 66
Prunus caroliana, 66
see also Carolina laurel cherry
Pumpkins, 154
Purple-leaf plum, 50, *50*

Race Track pansies, 104
Rancho Santa Ana Botanic Garden, 118
Ranunculus, *21*, 50, *108*
Raoulia, *141*
'Really Green' nicotiana, *135*
Recirculating pumps, 149
'Red Baron' peach trees, 150, *153*
Red lettuce, *150*
Redwood for trellises, 76
Redwoods, 81
Redwood soil amendment (RSA), 161
Reflecting pools, *10*
Refrigeration of bulbs, 109
Reinelt, Frank, 60
Rhizoctonia (fungus), 107
Robinson, William, 85
Rocks, 138–139
with bulbs, 110
in wildflower garden, 118
Rocky soils, 160–161
testing for, 163
Roger's Gardens (nursery), 103, 107
Roominess, 53, 54
for bulbs, 109
for flowering plants, 88
for hedges, 73
in kitchen gardens, 153
see also Open spaces
Root-bound plants, 167
Roots
air and drainage for, 160–161
holes for, *167*
number of, 168
of trees and shrubs, 77, 160, 161
see also Bare-root planting; Root-bound plants
Rosemary, 85
Roses, 19, *22*, *30*, 31–32, 64, *85*, 89–90, 99, *99*,
124, 129, 131, *133*, 167
see also Climbing roses
Rosmini, Christine, 42, 94, 129, *129*, 140
Rotary tiller, 163, *163*, 164
'Rotundifolium' Japanese privet, 66
Round Table delphiniums, 61
Roundup (herbicide), 116, 164, 166
RSA (redwood soil amendment), 161
Ruby violas, 104
Rule of three's and five's, 15, 54–55, 90, 145

Sackville-West, Victoria, 86, 129
Saffron, 112–113, *113*
Sage, *149*
Salvia, *32*, *46*, 63, 64, 99, *99*, *124*
Sand
as base for paving, 35–36
for bulbs, 109
as soil amendment, 162
Sandy soils, 160–161, *161*
soil amendments for, 163
testing for, 163
Santa Ana winds, 19
Santa Anita racetrack, 103
Santa Barbara daisies, *14*
Santolina chamaecyparissus, *26*, 40

Santolina virens, *26*, 40
Sasanqua camellias, 68
Sassafras Nursery & Landscaping, *100*
Satsuki azaleas, 70–71, *71*
Sawdust, 161, 167
Scabiosa, 63, *129*
S. caucasica, 128
Scale in design, 56
Scale ruler, *16*
Schinus molle, 78
Sculpture, 139, 140, *141*
Sedum spectabile, *36*
Senecio cineraria, see Dusty miller
Senecio leucostachys, *131*
Sequoias, 81
Serratifolia, 73
Shade, *see* Shadows and shade
Shade map, 21, *22*
Shadows and shade, *22*, 72–73
for bulbs under birch trees, *21*
for camellias, 68
for Corsican hellebore, 134
and ground covers, 40
lengthening shadows, 21–22
for pansies and violas, 107
planning for, 21–22
and soil preparation, 160
summer sun-winter shade problem, 101
of trees, 77
for tulips, 110
Shakespeare's pansies, 104
Shasta daisies, *63*, 64, *126*, *129*
'Shiko-No-Kagami' Satsuki azaleas, *71*
'Shimsen' Satsuki azaleas, 71, *71*
Shirley poppies, *63*
Shrimp plant, 134, *135*
Shrubs
as background, 46–47, 53, 65–66
flowering, 53
as perennials, 91
room for, 53
sizes of, for variety, *57*
and soil preparation, 160, 161
and watering, 168
see also Hedges
Size, 54
of dawn redwoods, 81
of flower beds, *86*, 86–89
of flowering plants, 88
little plants, 138, 140
of Satsuki azaleas, 70–71
of shrubs, 65
of tree leaves, 78
of trees, 78
Slopes and hills
and cold air, *19*
north-side and south-side microclimates of, 18
see also Banana belts
Slow growth
of ginkgoes, 81
of stephanotis vine, 76
Smaus, Louis, 60
Snapdragons, *63*
Snow-in-summer, *127*
Soil amendments
amount of, 163
and bare-root planting, 168
for bulbs, 109
mixing of, with soil, 163–164
and moisture in soil, 162–163
and nutrients in soil, 163
ongoing need for, 166
for opening up "heavy" soils, 161
organic, for flowers, 161
for pansies and violas, 107
for perennials, 97

for plants between paving stones, 143
for shade plants, 73
testing for necessity of, 163
see also Fertilizer; Mulch; Peat moss
Soils
for bulbs, 109
for delphiniums, 64
for dianthus, 93
in informal garden, 34
moisture in, 162–163, 168
nutrients in, 163
for pansies and violas, 107
for perennials, 97
for plants between paving stones, 143
preparation of, 160–166, *161, 163*
for Satsuki azaleas, 71
temperature of, and mulch, 171
see also Acid soils; Clay soils; Rocky soils; Sandy
soils; Soil amendments
Solanum jasminoides, 85
see also Potato vine
'Soleil d'Or' narcissus, 111, *111*
Southern California
climate of valleys and hills in, 18–19
collectibles in, 145
colors in, 123
fruit trees in, 150
impatiens in, 101
Santa Ana winds in, 19
shadows and shade in, 21–22
tulips in, 109
vines in, 75–76
wildflowers in, 117
South side of house, *19*
microclimate of, 18
Spa, with wildflowers, 118, *119*
Space, *see* Open spaces; Roominess
Spades, *171*
for dividing perennials, 97
for soil preparation, *161*
mixing in soil amendments, 163
Sphagnum moss, *10*
Spires, 57
Sporting, of Satsuki azaleas, 71
St. Augustine grass, 38
St. Catherine's lace, *131*
Stachys byzantina, see Lamb's ears
Staghorn ferns, 145
Staking, *168,* 171
Star jasmine, 32, *32*
Statice, *32*
Steele's pansies, 104
Steeples, 57
Steer manure, 161
Stephanotis, 128
S. floribunda, 75–76, *76*
Steps, of Palos Verdes stones, *14*
Stinkbugs, 171
Stock, 68, *91,* 101
Stones, 138–139
see also Pebbles; Rocks; Straddlestones
Straddlestones, 48, *48, 50*
Strawberries, 153
Streams, 149
Streptocarpus, *48*
Subshrubs, 91
Succulents, *10,* 140, *141*
Summer
flowers for, 19
shadows and shade in, 21–22, *22*
watering in, in California, 166
Summer Skies delphiniums, 60
Sunflowers, 154
Sunken gardens, 14
Sunlight
and gray foliage, 126

for kitchen gardens, 153
for pansies and violas, 107
planning for, 19–21
summer sun–winter shade problem, 101
see also Shadows and shade
Sun rose, *85*
Sunset Western Garden Book, 18, 54
Sun Valley, California, 115
Supports for vines, 76
Surprise, 57–58, *58*
'Suwanee River' Japanese privet, 66
'Sweet Afton' rose, 129
Sweet alyssum, 99, *99,* 146, *147*
'Sweet Memory' dianthus, *93*
Sweet pea, *144*
Sweet-smelling laurustinus, *67*
Sweet William, *63*
Swings, 139
Swiss chard, *150*

Tags, *171*
Tall fescues, 38, *41*
Telephone poles, hiding of, 46
Temperature
cold air, 18
of soil, and mulch, 171
see also Heat
'Texanum' Japanese privet, 66
Theodore Payne Foundation, 115
Thistle sage, 115
Thompson & Morgan, 103
Three's and five's, rule of, *see* Rule of three's
and five's
Thyme, *41, 93,* 143
Tidytips, 115, 118, *118*
Tiles, *36*
Tomatoes, 153, *154*
Topiary, 139
Trachelium, 63
Trees, 76–78, *78*
as backgrounds, 46
and bulbs, 108
and cold air, 18
and soil preparation, 160, 161
staking of, *168*
and watering, 168
Trellises
for beans and cucumbers, 154
for grape vines, 150
in informal gardens, 34
for vines, 76, *76*
for white heliotrope, 128
Trowels, *161, 171*
Tulips, *21, 22, 100,* 109–111
'Tulip Time' camellias, *69*
Turner's Variegated Dwarf pittosporum, 54

Umbrella frame, 50

Vegetables, 150–153, *163*
Verbascum chaixii, 128, *129*
Verbena rigida, 43, 95, 143
Veronica, 64, *97,* 110
Viburnum, 66
see also Laurustinus
Views and backgrounds, 47
Vinca rosea, 99
Vines, 74–76
Viola hederacea, 143
Violas, 103, *104,* 104–107
Violet Queen pansies, 103
Violets, *see* Violas
Walkways, *see* Paths
Walls, *14,* 73–74
as backgrounds, 46, 53, 99
of broken concrete, *95*

in flower beds, *88*
for kitchen gardens, 153
of Palos Verdes stones, *14, 15*
Watering, 168
amount of, 167
in California, 166, 168
in containers for plants, 145, 169
of daffodil bulbs, 108
of flower beds with bulbs, 110
of ground covers, 40
of lawns, 38
of pansies and violas, 107
before planting, 164
with watering basins, *164*
see also Soils, moisture in
Watering basins, *164*
Water in the garden, 149–150
Water lilies, 150
Watsonias, 61, 94, 95
Weeding fork, *161, 171*
Weeds and weeding
in ground covers, 40
in lawns, 38
and mulches, 171
between paving stones, 143
before planting, 164–166
with wildflowers, 115–117
Western Hills Nursery, 15
'Wheeler's Dwarf' pittosporum, *22, 72,* 73
White heliotrope, 129, *129*
White lantana, 129
White vinca, *99*
White yarrow, 128
Whitney, Lew, 103, 107
Wickson, E. J., 103
Wildflowers, 115–118, *116*
Window boxes, 107
Winds, 19
Winter shadows and shade, 21–22, *22*
Wisteria, *32,* 75
Woolly yarrow, *143*

Yarrow, 90, 128, *129,* 132, 143, *143*
Yellow-flowered gazanias, *131*
Yellow Queen pansies, 103
Yucca, 144

Zephyranthes grandiflora, 143
Zinnias, 99, *99,* 100, *100,* 110, 144
Zoysias, 38

PICTURE CREDITS

Photograph and illustration credits are listed here
by page number.

Glen Allison: 27, 35, 42, 43, 61, 62–63, 100, 101,
140 all, 141; Martha Auckland: 39; George de
Gennaro: 110, 111, 169; Richard Fish: 98; John
Reed Foresman: 29, 90; Christina Giesenfeld: 18,
22, 30, 47, 161, 166; Mary Ellen Guffey: 105, 106
all, 133, 151; Peter Hogg: 134, 135 all; Rosemary
Kaul: 23, 146–47; R. B. Leffingwell: 33, 34, 81 all;
Jack Nelson: 44–45, 80; Kathlene Persoff: 1–5, 8–
9, 11, 12–13, 14, 15, 20, 24–25, 28, 31, 32, 36, 41,
48, 49, 50–51, 52, 59, 66 all, 67 all, 69 all, 70, 71
all, 72, 79, 82–83, 84, 87, 89, 94–95, 99, 102, 108,
114 all, 116, 117, 119, 122, 125, 131, 136–37, 145, 148,
158–59; Susan Ragsdale: 154–55, 156–57; Wayne
Shimabukuro: 37; Robert Smaus: 17, 55, 56, 58, 73
all, 74, 77, 92 all, 93, 96 all, 113, 120–21, 126, 127,
128 all, 129, 130, 132, 139, 142, 143, 144, 152, 162,
165, 170.